ECONOMICS OF SCIENTIFIC JOURNALS

Ad Hoc Committee on Economics of Publication:

Other books published by the Council of Biology Editors, Inc.

CBE Style Manual, 4th edition. 1978, reprinted 1982
Scientific Writing for Graduate Students. 1968, reprinted 1976, 1981

ECONOMICS OF SCIENTIFIC JOURNALS

Edited by

AD HOC COMMITTEE ON ECONOMICS OF PUBLICATION

D. H. Michael Bowen, *Chairman*

PUBLISHED BY

COUNCIL OF BIOLOGY EDITORS, INC.

BETHESDA, MARYLAND

1982

Library of Congress Cataloging in Publication Data
Main entry under title:

Economics of scientific journals.

    1. Science—Periodicals—Publishing—Economic
aspects. I. Council of Biology Editors. Committee
on Economics of Publication.
Z286.S4E258   1982   338.4′7505   82–19926

ISBN: 0–914340–03–4

CONTENTS

PREFACE

In 1973, the Council of Biology Editors published the proceedings of a workshop entitled "Economics of Scientific Publications," which had been held earlier that year. Since that time, the Board of Directors has focused on this very important subject with a view to publishing a sequel to the proceedings. In the intervening years, several symposia held at CBE meetings dealt with the various aspects of the economics of scientific publishing.

This book is based in large part on papers originally presented at a symposium chaired by Harry Williamson in 1977; several papers presented at subsequent CBE symposia are also included. All papers have been thoroughly updated or rewritten where appropriate. We make no claim of total comprehensiveness or absolute consistency for the contents; however, we believe that this book contains valuable information that will be of help to CBE members and to scientific editors and publishers who need to grapple with economic problems in these trying financial times.

We invite our readers to comment on the contents and to suggest topics for future CBE symposia, workshops, or a possible manual on the subject of economics of publishing.

We are all indebted to the authors for sharing their knowledge and to an ad hoc committee on economics of publication that made a concerted effort to bring this book to completion. Members of the committee were: D. H. Michael Bowen, chairman; Joanne Fetzner; Gisella Pollock; Jeffrey Watson; and Philip Altman, ex officio. Copy editing was done by Laurie Chambers. This preface would be incomplete without acknowledgment of the sterling efforts of Gisella Pollock, who has coordinated all aspects of final processing and production. She has brought a very necessary sense of order, urgency, and professionalism to this all-volunteer effort.

D. H. Michael Bowen
Chairman
CBE Committee on Economics of Publication

CONTRIBUTORS

D. H. MICHAEL BOWEN
Director
Books & Journals Division
American Chemical Society
Washington, DC 20036

MARGARET BROADBENT
Consultant for Publishing
The Rockefeller Archives
Pocantico Hills, North Tarrytown
New York 10591
Formerly:
Manager Journals Office
Rockefeller University Press

JOANNE FETZNER
Managing Editor, *Psychophysiology*
Society for Psychophysiological Research
2380 Lisa Lane
Madison, Wisconsin 53711

ROY C. FLETCHER
Controller
Chamber of Commerce of the U.S.
Washington, DC 20062
Formerly:
Controller
American Society for Microbiology

LEWIS I. GIDEZ
Executive Editor
Journal of Lipid Research
Albert Einstein College of Medicine
Bronx, New York 10461

CHARLES C. HANCOCK
Executive Officer
Journal of Biological Chemistry
American Society of Biological Chemists
Bethesda, Maryland 20814

SAMUEL G. MACFARLANE
Vice President, Finance
Waverly Press, Inc.
Baltimore, Maryland 21202

ROBERT H. MARKS
Associate Director for Publishing
American Institute of Physics
New York, New York 10017

ROBERT V. ORMES
Associate Publisher, *Science*
American Association for the Advancement
of Science
Washington, DC 20005

MILTON C. PAIGE, JR.
Kennebunkport, Maine 04046
Formerly:
Business Manager
New England Journal of Medicine

JOHN R. RICE
Comptroller
Federation of American Societies for
Experimental Biology
Bethesda, Maryland 20814

GEORGE B. ROSCOE
Author, Consultant (Postal and
Magazine Management)
7910 West Boulevard Drive
Alexandria, Virginia 22308
Formerly:
Editor and Publisher
Electrical Contractor

EARL SCHERAGO
President, Scherago Associates
1515 Broadway
New York, New York 10036

MORNA CONWAY SCHMICK
President, Morna Conway, Inc.
P. O. Box 195
Woodbine, Maryland 21797

A. F. SPILHAUS, JR.
Executive Director
American Geophysical Union
Washington, DC 20009

Member Subscriptions

D. H. MICHAEL BOWEN

Members are the backbone of any society publishing program. Society members function as the initiators of new journals, as journal editors and associate editors, as reviewers and referees, and of course as authors. In most societies, they also act as the arbiters of the success or failure of journals and are heavily involved in publishing policy through service on society-wide publication committees or boards. By comparison, most nonmembers—even those who are faithful subscribers—have relatively little contact with the operation of society journals.

Editors of society journals are customarily members of the society, even though membership is probably not a formal requirement. Each may be paid a modest stipend, which is not meant to represent exact payment for hours of work rendered. In practice, the editorial work is subsidized by the editors and their institutions of employment, which often provide office space and perhaps secretarial help at little or no cost.

Studies have indicated that there is a great likelihood that at least one author of each paper published in society journals will be a member of the sponsoring society. Some specific studies performed within the American Chemical Society (ACS) indicate that well over half of its reviewers and referees are members; they are chosen as referees at least partly because they previously have authored papers in society journals.

Every year hundreds of thousands of manuscripts are submitted to scientific journals for review. Each manuscript is typically reviewed by two individuals, resulting in perhaps a million reviews annually. This impressive economic commitment on the part of the referees is rendered without remuneration. The uncompensated, voluntarily provided effort is consistent with the widely held and deeply ingrained belief of almost all research scientists that the peer review is a vitally important concept underlying the strength and integrity of science.

This preamble is necessary if the economic picture of an individual society journal system is to be seen in its proper context. It is easy to look on the role of the society member solely as a subscriber rather than as a contributor in other ways, such as those outlined above. The balance of this chapter is devoted to exploring the problems that result from extending subscription price privileges to members, to attract and retain them as subscribers.

The following situation is familiar to the publishers of all society journals, whether the journal is published by the society itself or by a commercial publisher on its behalf: Each year the number of member subscribers decreases; each succeeding year the price is raised, then the number of subscriptions decreases once more, until one day no more members subscribe. Most societies are anxious to avoid following this trend to its bitter end. Yet time and social habits are working against them. It is becoming less common for a scientist to feel obligated to possess the personal "tools of the trade." The price of these tools has of course risen, but even where it has not, there is evidence that many scientists are relying on subscriptions purchased by others. In most cases it is the institution of employment that has assumed the burden of supplying these tools, in much the same way as it provides the scientist with computer and laboratory facilities. Furthermore the traditional scientific journal is not a highly efficient vehicle for disseminating information to the individual scientist, who reads very few of the papers in any given issue, according to repeated studies.

From the outset it must be recognized that it is unrealistic to expect revenue from member subscriptions to make any great contribution to the financial viability of an individual society journal or group of journals. Costs have risen to such a degree that were a society to ask all subscribers, member and nonmember alike, to pay equal prices, members would be driven out of the market. Member subscribers are very sensitive to price; though the degree of price sensitivity varies with the field of the journal, in general, higher subscription prices almost invariably result in fewer subscribers. Therefore society publishers should not raise subscription prices to members unless absolutely necessary and unless they are prepared for a circulation decline.

Of course under certain conditions member subscription prices must be increased. When revenue from member subscriptions fails to cover the cost of running another copy off the press, wrapping it, mailing it, and servicing the subscription out of a fulfillment system, member subscriptions are actually losing money. Few societies would wish to be in such a position without some compensating source of revenue, such as advertising, and then must beware of the tax implications (see below). The general rule of thumb among most professional and scientific publishers is to have member subscription revenue at least cover runoff cost plus subscription fulfillment cost. Over recent years, the costs of paper and postage have increased markedly and therefore have contributed to an unusually large increase in runoff costs. A society that assumes it is covering these costs with member subscription revenue may not in fact be doing so, and a detailed check is advisable.

Adoption of a guideline specifying that the member subscription price will cover runoff and fulfillment cost for one member subscription means in practice that a society intends to recover all front-end costs, such as redaction, typesetting, camera work, stripping, and overhead, from nonmember subscribers. The practical consequence of this philosophy is that nonmember prices need to be several times higher than member prices, a source of some potential difficulties that are explored below. A positive aspect of a large difference between member and nonmember prices is that it provides a powerful incentive for a suitably qualified individual to join the society. If the differential is large enough, sometimes it exceeds the cost of membership dues. This is an authentic inducement to join the society that cannot be overemphasized when listing membership benefits to qualified nonmember individuals. On the other side of the coin, however, the member/nonmember price difference leads in practice to widespread "cheating." Cheating is the purchase by a nonmember of a subscription in the name of a member to save on subscription costs. This problem is not entirely tractable and can produce some unfortunate confrontations between society and member, which the ACS has tried to counter in several ways. First, all new ACS members are required to sign a declaration on the membership application form that any subscriptions purchased at the special member rate will be solely for personal use. Second, the computer-generated member dues and subscription billing card has a paragraph set in red type that reminds the member of the personal-use restriction. No signature is called for on this dues card. Third, print runs of ACS basic journals are arranged in two separate segments, one for members and one for nonmembers. The two segments are provided with different covers at the final stage of binding. The cover intended for a member has the personal-use restriction stated quite visibly. Although ACS has never directly attempted to enforce compliance with the restriction—attempts to do so would constitute poor member and subscriber relations and would be totally unfeasible—some evidence suggests that the cover restriction is helpful in reducing cheating. When nonmembers were once inadvertently provided with copies of *The Journal of Organic Chemistry* having member covers, many librarians from around the country were distraught at the prospect of displaying such a cover on library shelves and called ACS to resolve the problem.

A very practical consideration in the member/nonmember price differential is that the U.S. Postal Service has some influence, as it does in a surprisingly large number of other matters of concern to nonprofit publishers. Under U.S.P.S. regulation 132.228, no subscriber is allowed to pay less than half of the base rate if the publisher is to enjoy second-class nonprofit postage rates on that journal. Most publishers can live with this restriction by ensuring that the base rate for each of their publications is the member rate, not the nonmember rate. Also they must be careful that students and any others being charged very low rates do not pay less than half the member rate. Note, however, that the postal service, not the publisher, has the last word in such matters.

U.S. Internal Revenue Service (IRS) regulations govern the assessment of taxes on unrelated business income to nonprofit organiztions. Specific, but lengthy, rules explain how a society should allocate monies from members' dues for subscriptions to any publications members receive as part of their dues. Societies having such publications should be aware of these regulations and should obtain competent tax advice.

At one time there was reason to believe that the IRS viewed a large differential between member and nonmember subscription prices as inurement of nonmember monies to the illegal benefit of members. A case concerning this matter was brought against ACS by the IRS. However, it was settled out of court in 1980, with the IRS admitting that the pricing of subscriptions to members and nonmembers has no bearing whatsoever on the tax-exempt status of the society.

Of course, raising prices to nonmembers is no financial panacea. For one thing, not all nonmember subscribers are institutions, and individual nonmembers are just as sensitive to price increases as are members. The result of several years of raising nonmember prices has been almost total elimination of individual nonmember subscribers. It is possible to counter this result to some extent by adopting a three-tier subscription price structure in which the middle tier is the nonmember individual price, intermediate between the member price and the nonmember institutional price. Currently many institutions are under financial constraints, with declining or at best steady acquisition budgets. No longer can a publisher take it for granted that an institution or library will automatically subscribe to a new journal or even continue to subscribe to existing journals. Librarians tend to resent the special price break given by societies to their members. Publishers of society-sponsored journals should take care when setting prices to ensure that the difference in price charged to members and to institutions is not so large as to provide a disincentive for institutions to subscribe. It is possible to offer low rates to members only if there are sufficient nonmember subscribers to cover the major portion of front-end cost.

In summary, it can be said that members of a society are of inestimable value to a publications program but that members are going to be very difficult to retain as subscribers. A knowledge of the exact cost related to producing and fulfilling member subscriptions is a necessary prerequisite to drawing up a policy regarding pricing of journals to members. I believe that pricing at or slightly above runoff cost plus fulfillment costs makes the best sense. An attempt to have members absorb a significant fraction of front-end cost may be self-defeating as members drop subscriptions when faced with much higher subscription prices. If and when society journals reach the point where they have no personal subscribers whatsoever—either members or nonmembers—a certain spark will have left the scientific journals business, perhaps forever. On the other hand, it is not financially feasible for society publishers to accept a situation in which subscriptions purchased at low member prices substitute for library subscriptions purchased at a much higher rate. That situation seems more of a probability now that library budgets are severely strained than it did 10 years ago. It is going to take real ingenuity to balance, through appropriate price setting, the legitimate interests of both members and institutions.

Over the longer term, it will be essential for all journal publishers to rethink the journal business as it affects members and other individuals. The printed journal of today is a rather cumbersome way to provide information to an individual. Experiments with selective dissemination of information and synoptic journals, and with on-line access to the contents of journals, may point the way to better and more cost-effective methods.

Single Issues and Back Volumes

S. G. MACFARLANE

The sale of single issues and back volumes of scientific journals is essentially a service operation, subsidiary to the main business of providing communication to the scientific community via subscriptions to the journals. Nevertheless, it is an important service to the customers who have need for it, and there is no reason why it should not be profitable to the publisher or at least self-supporting. The key elements of profitability are marketing, pricing, inventory control, and fulfillment cost control.

The important element in marketing is to realize that for back volumes and for most single issues no marketing expense needs to be incurred. The publisher has no influence over the demand for these products; it exists, and the publisher is the first source to which the potential customer turns. Special issues are an exception. They are, by their nature, of interest to a greater audience than the body of regular subscribers and deserve some modest promotional expenditures. The most economical marketing effort is a notice in the journal itself (house advertisement), run in the issues preceding and following the special issue. A more ambitious program is to run advertisements in other journals whose audiences are appropriate for the special issue. The cost of such a program often can be minimized by arrangements to exchange advertisements. A third approach is the use of direct mail to audiences other than the journal's own subscribers. This type of effort is usually not cost justified unless some products in addition to the single issue are to be promoted in the same mailing. For example, a mailing promoting subscriptions to the journal itself could well include mention of special issue(s) of the journal to be published or previously issued.

It is convenient to keep the back volume price the same as the current subscription price. This automatically keeps the back volume price current with inflation. Even though the issues were manufactured at historic cost levels, cost of storage and order fulfillment (including postage) will have tended to increase on an annual basis. An exception to this pricing philosophy is appropriate when the size of the journal (number of text pages) increases dramatically over a period of time. In this instance it is sensible to have more than one price level for back volumes, with the price breaks coinciding with the change in journal size.

Pricing of regular single issues is most easily accomplished by dividing the subscription price by the number of issues, adding a premium for small-order cost recovery, and rounding up to the next even dollar. The premium may be a flat dollar amount ($1.00–$3.00) or a percentage (25%, 50%, etc.). This will minimize the publisher's theoretical loss on the sale of single copies without drastically penalizing the customer. Special issues should be priced higher than regular issues because of the inherently greater value of the issue and, in some cases, to support the cost of publicizing the special issue. The amount of premium for the special issue should take into consideration the greater size, if any, of the special issue and any extra editorial expense associated with it. If the journal has pricing differentials for its subscribers (domestic vs. foreign, individual vs. institutional), the differentials should carry over to prices for back volumes and single issues.

Inventory control starts with setting press runs and ends with warehouse inventory records. The press-run calculation should include an allowance for back volume sales, based on historical needs in the case of a mature journal. Historical needs can be measured most easily from examination of inventory records. The number of copies used from the end of the year of publication to the end of the period that you plan to keep back volumes available is the figure to be determined. With the exception of special issues, one can assume that the need for back issues will be uniform for all issues in the volume; it is not necessary to measure each regular issue in the volume. This presumes the existence of a policy about the length of time that back volumes will be maintained, which is best determined by the duration of reasonable demand for them after the year of publication. With proper pricing, it is economically feasible to maintain back volumes until annual demand falls below a half-dozen sets. Special issues require individual judgments about retention.

It is helpful to provide the journal's potential back volume customers with a source of supply even after the end of the period determined as feasible for provision of this service. Several commercial organizations are in this field, taking over remaining inventory on either an outright sale or consignment basis. In the latter case, the back issue dealer pays royalties on sales of back volumes. In either instance the dealer customarily pays the freight charges for transfer of the inventory; the dealer usually has the right to reprice the issues and to reprint the issues, if warranted by demand. If plans include eventual disposition to a dealer, it is appropriate to plan on printing enough copies to allow for his usual order. The appetite of the back issue dealers for this overstock has diminished in recent years, probably because of the availability of microfilm and other forms of archival storage.

Since back volume storage is a real cost, either to the printer or to the publisher, it is vital to dispose of excess stock as soon as possible after publication. Normally this might be done for the whole volume one year after the year of publication, based on a current inventory record. If the printer has abnormally low spoilage on a particular issue, resulting in an excessive number of overcopies to begin with, the excess should be destroyed immediately so that storage costs are nipped in the bud. Conversely, abnormally high spoilage may result in the decision to reprint an issue, as a service to customers, even though it is not apt to be cost justified. Because the published material in a scientific journal is available in other forms, such as microfilm, the publisher should not feel the need or responsibility to maintain back volumes ad infinitum. Indeed, most publishers are experiencing declining unit, if not dollar, sales of back volumes, attributable for the most part to alternative sources for previously published material.

Brief mention should be made of back volume inventory planning for a new journal. Since the building of subscriptions for a new journal usually takes place over several years, it is good business and good customer service to overprint the first and second years' issues in anticipation of some demand for the issues by new subscribers in the third and fourth years of publication. Do not expect that all or even most of those third- and fourth-year subscribers will want the back volumes, however.

Order fulfillment for single issues and back volumes is normally an adjunct to subscription fulfillment. It is useful to know about how much clerical time is required so that the costs of the back volume and single issue service operation can be measured against the income it produces. Only a few basics should be mentioned regarding fulfillment. The person responsible needs to know issue availability (inventory status), current prices, and billing policy. Payment in advance is recommended to reduce the clerical overhead associated with this relatively low-yield service. A current price and availability list can be produced at low cost and used to answer inquiries from potential customers; payment terms should be included on this form. It should also indicate the availability of older issues from the back issue dealer, if any, who services the journal.

A final word should be said about the place of back volume and single issue sales in overall financial planning of a scientific journal. Income from this operation should be considered a fringe benefit and not be counted on to support the editorial and manufacturing cost structure of the journal. It is for most journals a relatively insignificant and declining source of income. It should be subject to limited cost accounting to ensure that it is run on a profitable or break-even basis. In this regard, manufacturing costs of overcopies (back issue inventory) should be charged against, and supported by, subscription income. This is not only financially sound but also avoids the problem of inventory cost records for these overcopies. Income should be compared to the costs of storage, order fulfillment, mailing, and promotion, if any, to keep the operation in proper perspective.

Reprints

Charles C. Hancock

Reprints are reproductions of individual articles printed in a composite publication such as a primary journal. They are sold to authors and, depending on journal policy, to others. Their sale can represent a significant source of income to a journal publisher. On the other hand, a number of publishers of primary journals, principally in the ranks of commercial publishers, regularly give complimentary reprints to authors. Under these circumstances, the number so offered is limited but the author has the option of ordering additional copies, frequently at nominal cost.

Reprints are usually supplied in the same format as in the journal, although some publishers occasionally supply different sizes prepared by photoreduction or photoenlargement. Some publishers still supply reprints with covers that may be custom imprinted with the title of the communication, the authors, and the laboratory of origin, although this practice is decreasing. Other publishers supply reprints with covers having die-cut windows, but these are fragile and are frequently damaged in storage or in filing.

The economics of reprint are significantly influenced by journal makeup. They may be printed quite conveniently by an overrun system during the printing of the journal. This is especially true if the journal style calls for every article to begin on a right-hand page. Enough extra impressions are printed during the journal press run to satisfy the reprint order. The folded signatures are torn apart and stapled to include only the particular article.

The overrun of each signature is determined by the largest reprint order in the particular signature. Therefore a large order for a short article that is tucked in a 32-page signature can result in sizable wastage. In addition the overrun system can result in a significant number of blank pages, i.e., the last page will be blank in about 50% of the cases, as in the actual journal. Whether the cost of blank pages and wastage is offset by the saving from not having to reimpose has to be determined. Where journal style calls for each item to begin on a new page (either right or left), some reimposition is required to manufacture the reprints of, on the average, three-quarters of the items, since half will start on a right-hand page and half will end on a left-hand page and only that 25% starting on a right-hand page and ending on a left-hand page will require no reimposition.

For the journals that fail to start each new item on a new page, either right or left, either extensive reimposition is required or the reprints produced by the overrun method will lack a certain grace and elegance since parts of the preceding or succeeding articles will accompany the reprint. Regardless of the method used, there must be trade-offs determined by careful consideration of costs and of the price schedules for reprints sold to authors or others.

Some printers have special equipment that allows them to manufacture reprints by making electrostatic plates from the regular journal run and using these on small presses. Each article is separately reimposed to print four-page signatures in two passes. These are then collated, folded, saddle-stitched, and trimmed. This method is not universally applicable, since its use is limited by page size and press run. Where it can be applied it speeds up the production and shipment of reprints.

Publisher policy determines whether the sale of reprints is limited to authors or whether large runs of reprints are supplied to commercial organizations whose products are mentioned in a given article. Publisher policy also determines whether the number of reprints sold is to be limited and what rights are given to authors for subsequent reprinting. The latest copyright law also affects the rights of authors. If the journal does not own an exclusive copyright to the individual articles, the author(s) can reproduce the article in any amount. Usually such reprinting is not economical for an initial supply of reprints, but additional copies can be reproduced locally without going back to the publisher. The quality of local reproduction may not be as high as the original, especially for figures other than line drawings, but this is a judgment that must be made by the author(s).

Publisher policy determines the markup to be applied to reprints, regardless of how they are made, and this in turn is a major factor in determining how lucrative their sale can be. Markup can vary from 0% to over 100% of the cost to the publisher for manufacturing the reprints. Markup may also depend on the number of pages of the original article, the quantity ordered, and whether covers are to be supplied. Even at the higher prices it is assumed that authors will want reprints to distribute to their colleagues. There is also a philosophical consideration in determining markup. Since overall journal income can come from several sources, such as from libraries for subscriptions, from individuals for subscriptions, and from authors for page charges and reprints, the publisher can determine a balance of these sources. If little or no markup is charged for reprints, subscriptions will need to be higher to meet the desired profit margin. A higher markup will reduce the subscription price, thereby encouraging more subscriptions or taking pressure off tight library budgets.

Some publishers sell individual reprints on demand. However, this raises inventory problems and there is a current tendency to displace this practice by contracting with service organizations to supply individual reprints on demand by using modern reprographic techniques. Some of these services are operated by "for-profit" organizations. The copyright law should again be considered, since the publisher cannot authorize reprinting of the article if the copyright has not been transferred to the publisher.

Reprints can be intrinsically expensive and the costs of their subsequent handling can quickly elevate them into the luxury category. An individual requesting a reprint sustains the expense of making the request and paying postage for it; the recipient of the request must meet the cost of the reprint plus the cost of addressing and mailing a copy back to the requester. In a laboratory that is judged productive because of the number of publications emanating from it, the maintenance and use of reprint mailing lists and the fulfillment of reprint requests can easily occupy a full-time clerical assistant.

Although most publishers require that orders for reprints be placed at the time at which galley or page proof is returned, publishers can be dilatory in fulfilling reprint orders and shipping reprints to their purchasers. Consequently it is not uncommon for reprint requests to accumulate with the author well in advance of the receipt of reprints. This situation is aggravated by the habit that many individuals have developed of requesting reprints from listings in such publications as *Current Contents*. At best the time delay between the mailing of a request and the receipt of the reprint from the author can be long enough so that when the reprint arrives the requester will often have forgotten that it had been ordered.

This situation, coupled with the increased availability of comparatively inexpensive photoreproduction equipment, has contributed to the growing tendency of individual researchers to make copies of articles in which they are interested without writing for reprints and waiting for their receipt. As the cost of photoreproduction decreases and the quality of photocopies improves, the tendency to follow this practice will grow. The use of reprints could ultimately become limited to those instances where information transfer requires the highest quality reproduction of halftones, electron micrographs, and the like and where high-quality products are needed for grant proposals, etc. When high-quality reproduction is a prime consideration, reprints must be supplied on the same quality paper as used in the journal, and photoreproduction would not be possible.

Where data are available, it is useful for the publisher to calculate the net reprint income per text page published or per item published. In this way a judgment can be made of the trend of reprint income with time over a period of years on a normalized basis. In the absence of such comparative data, it is difficult to generalize and estimate future budgets.

Because so many factors enter into the cost of reprint production, it is important to isolate these costs and offset them against gross reprint sales to obtain reliable estimates of net reprint income. It is important to include the cost of invoicing, follow-up against institutional purchase orders, packing and shipping of reprints, and the like. It has proved convenient and practical, in some instances, to price reprints based on increments of two pages and in quantities of 100's.

Regardless of the economic considerations, reprints clearly are, and will continue to be, a significant source of income to a journal publisher, and this income can be obtained with little or no effort. On the other hand, if costs are not carefully analyzed, a publisher can end up subsidizing authors for their reprints. Journal policy must be defined to establish the "what" and "why" of reprints. Is the publisher's chief concern to facilitate communication or to derive income for the journal? Are reprints to be supplied as a service to those desiring to promote goods or equipment? Should reprints be supplied on a complimentary basis or at very low cost to attract authors? These unrelated questions need to be considered carefully in the formulation of journal policy before ground rules are set and price structures determined. In all circumstances, substantial efforts must be expended to ensure the prompt manufacture and delivery of reprints.

This chapter is based on an initial draft by the late R. A. Harte.

Advertising in Scholarly Journals

EARL J. SCHERAGO

Someone once said that golf is a game in which one attempts to strike a small white sphere with tools patently ill-suited for the task. Selling advertising space in scholarly journals presents a somewhat similar problem because it is an attempt to sell a product, without the proper tools, to people who do not wish to buy. It is a strange paradox that both the publishers of scientific journals and their prospective advertisers see space advertising as a necessary evil. The editors of the journal reluctantly accept it because it ultimately becomes necessary for the existence of the journal, and the advertiser resists buying it because he is never really convinced that it pays off in terms of product sales. Both exhibit a considerable amount of naivety about the objectives of the other, a fact that makes the whole procedure extremely difficult.

The sale of advertising space is one of the most competitive enterprises in our society. It is the only business in which competitors must continually advertise to each other the identity of their customers. Because of the mystique connected with it, scholarly journal editors usually approach advertising with a completely distorted idea of what is involved.

Once the traumatic decision has been made to accept advertising in a journal, many editors believe that they need merely to announce the fact to the business community and the contracts will start flowing in. Because they inject so much of themselves into producing the high-quality editorial package typical of scholarly journals, they assume that advertisers will be standing in line breathlessly awaiting the opportunity to buy space in the publication. Unfortunately the journalistic graveyard is littered with publications that, having made the painful decision to accept advertising as a last financial resort, fail to appreciate the fact that the advertiser is a paying customer who has to be wooed.

If an editor is not ready to exhibit some humility, respect the advertiser's right to want to sell his product, and recognize that advertisers are not operating charitable, nonprofit enterprises, then he should forget the whole idea. This is not to say that he is going to sell his editorial soul to the business devil. It does mean he must keep an open mind and block out temporarily some traditional scholarly publishing attitudes.

As mentioned before, the sale of advertising is a highly competitive business.

An editor might well then ask, with whom shall I compete? To answer that question, we must examine the three main types of publications circulated to scientists.

TYPES OF SCIENTIFIC PUBLICATIONS

Commercial Scholarly or Scientific Journals

These are journals often published by book publishers that usually practice traditional peer review; their editorial content is controlled by an active independent editorial board. Editorial material consists of original research usually accepted as archival knowledge. The publishers of this type of journal hope to make their profits from subscriptions, and consequently they must keep their editorial content of high quality. Circulation is usually very small because of the high subscription price that the publisher must charge to make a profit. Formats are usually scholarly in nature, small in size (6 × 8½ in.), and relatively dull in appearance as far as advertisers are concerned. These journals usually carry little advertising because it is not seen as the primary source of revenue. Also, the principal subscribers are libraries, which are of no interest to advertisers.

Association or Society Scholarly or Scientific Journals

Society journals are essentially the same as those above except that most subscriptions come from an allotment of society dues. Nonmember subscriptions originate mainly from libraries and institutions. Society journals also frequently have substantial student subscriptions because of discount rates to that group. In general, library and student subscriptions are of no interest to advertisers and are considered a liability.

Controlled Free-Circulation Journals (Throwaways)

This type of publication constitutes the primary competition for advertising for peer review scholarly journals. As a group, they own about 80% of the advertising sales market because they operate under no scientific ethical restrictions. Consequently, they are far more flexible with respect to advertisers' wishes. Controlled circulation journals exhibit two main differences from scholarly journals. First, their primary objective is to sell advertising rather than subscriptions. Second, the reader can take no remedial action to express dissatisfaction with the quality and type of editorial content, because he has not paid for his subscription. When a throwaway enters a field of scientific activity, it takes two actions: 1) it accumulates or locates for rental a list of all scientists in the given area and 2) it compiles a list of prospective advertisers often derived from the advertisers in the scholarly journals. The editorial content in throwaways is usually of no scientific (archival) value, since hardly any of them use a scientifically valid peer review editorial system. Usually the articles are selected by lay editors who have no scientific training. Many retain prestigious editorial boards that actually have little or no control over the editorial material. Often articles are written by advertisers or commissioned by advertisers. In addition, these journals invariably publish "new product" releases that are free advertisements and that often are selected on the basis of attracting advertisers rather than of having value to the reader. Most controlled circulation publications use a reader service card (called "Bingo Card" in the trade), which offers the advertiser a tangible evaluation of the results of his advertising. In general, the editors and publishers of throwaways feel no responsibility for scientific style and tradition. In fact, they see scholarly journals as poor editorial packages, unattractive in format and dull to read. Since the people who buy and influence the purchase of advertising are rarely scientists, they have no understanding of the importance of peer review journals to scientists. The scientific community, on the other hand, because it is for the most part unaware of the vast amounts of advertising dollars drained away from scholarly journals by throwaways, has remained impassive about the threat that throwaways represent for scholarly peer review journals. This situation quite likely will prevail for some time despite the efforts of Abelson and Ormes (1), Scherago (2), and King (3) to enlighten scientists concerning the problem. Controlled circulation non–peer review journals might logically be compared with television, where the advertiser also pays the cost of production and distribution. As a group, TV advertisers determine the type and quality of shows that are aired and each specific advertiser has considerable control over the material in the shows he sponsors. Obviously, such practices are diametrically opposed to all the principles of peer review publishing.

HOW ADVERTISING IS BOUGHT

Advertising space is bought as a result of effort by a team composed of the advertiser and the advertising agency. The team usually has at least four members: the advertising manager at the company, the company product or sales manager, the media buyer at the advertising agency, and the account executive. The relative influence of each varies considerably with the type of advertiser involved (product, recruiting, corporate, etc.) and with the size of the company. Generally, the larger the company, the more influential the agency. The procedure normally starts with a recommendation from the media buyer. The account executive then approves the media list submitted by the buyer. The schedule is then shown to the advertising manager for the client, who then goes over it with the company product or marketing manager. Any one of the individuals involved can cut a magazine off the schedule, and therefore the magazine must be "sold" to all individuals involved. Furthermore, one never knows with which individual the decision will rest, since the flow may go from client to agency in some cases. The situation may be complicated even more by each individual placing great emphasis on entirely different factors. The agency people may be more interested in graphics and image, whereas the client may be more interested in inquiries and circulation. Added to this is a variation in individual tastes and prejudices: i.e., some agencies do not like society publications, most do not like journal format, and everyone objects to the bunching of advertising. Most journals do not mingle editorial matter and advertising; ad pages are "bunched" at the front and/or back of an issue. Ninety percent of all advertising is bought for a company's entire fiscal year, three months before its beginning. Thus, if one wishes to obtain a contract from a specific agency, the selling must be done in the year preceding the time a commitment is made by the advertiser. It is virtually impossible to obtain advertising from an advertising agency once it has made up the advertising schedule of its client for the fiscal year. Ironically, however, the contract issued by an advertising agency concerning the advertising to be placed for its client during the fiscal year is not binding. It may be amended up or down and often is canceled entirely. The contract in effect serves to identify the publications in which an advertiser intends to place space and constitutes a vague promise to place a specific amount of space. The insertion order is the actual order for a specific advertisement in a specific issue. A publication cannot run an advertisement until it receives this document.

FACTORS AFFECTING THE SALE OF ADVERTISING

• Bulk or Thickness. Advertisers and agencies do not like thin magazines. Thickness to them is a sign of success and acceptance of the publication.

• Advertisers Already "In." Advertisers like to play follow the leader. If one can sell 2 out of 6 advertisers in any given field on a regular basis, one will soon have them all. The total number of advertisers is all-important in that it indicates the acceptance of the publication on the part of advertisers of all kinds.

• Audited Statement. Most agencies will not even look at a publication whose circulation statement is not audited by one of the accepted auditing agencies. These are: Business Publications Audit of Circulation, Inc.; Audit Bureau of Circulations; and Verified Audit Circulation Corp. All of these audits are expensive. Audited statements are the agencies protection against fraudulent circulation claims by publishers.

• Graphics or Appearance. These qualities (other than bulk or thickness) are very important to agencies. Media buyers paradoxically have a tendency to buy space in magazines that they themselves would read, rather than in those that the advertiser's prospective customers would read. They revel in such things as four-color cover, four-color inside pages, plenty of art work and pictures, heavy expensive stock, pictures on covers, etc. For the most part they see scholarly journals as poor publishing packages.

• Circulation. The overall size of a publication's circulation is not as important as how well it covers the area of interest for the advertiser. For some advertisers a large circulation is a liability because it forces up the page rates. If an advertiser is not interested in all subscribers, he must determine the cost for only the people that he wishes to reach. In the advertising field this is called effective cost per thousand. Large circulations are helpful only where advertisers are interested in the entire community. Advertisers consider students, libraries, and institutions ineffective or waste circulation.

• Frequency. The frequency of publication is an important factor to some advertisers. Advertisers like to place space as soon as they have a need, and since demands rise and fall suddenly, the long lead time of a bimonthly may leave them with an advertisement scheduled at a time they do not want. In general, recruiters favor daily or weekly publications over monthly or bimonthly ones. To most advertising agencies bimonthly or quarterly publication means that a publisher does not have the funds to invest or enough advertisers to go monthly. This undermines confidence in a publication.

* Editorial Quantity. The quantity of a publication's editorial content is important to agencies. If it has few pages of editorial content, the agency may feel that there is not enough there to interest the reader. Advertisers in general like to see a 50:50 ratio of editorial material to advertising.

* Editorial Quality. The quality of the editorial content is important to agencies. They tend to favor such content that is easily readable and that they feel will be interesting to the reader. They tend to judge this based on what they themselves would read. Advertisers do not judge editorial quality in the same way a scientist does.

* Editorial Staff. Agencies tend to judge editorial material to some extent from the size of the editorial staff. The larger the editorial staff, the more prestige a publication enjoys.

* Image. All publications sooner or later develop an image. The image may be good or bad, but once it is established, it is virtually impossible to change it. Some kinds of images are *class publication, bingo book, journal, long hair, management book*. It is therefore important that the ultimate desired image be considered when a publication is soliciting advertising initially. Advertisers will develop their image of a magazine on the first presentation and will carry it for some time even though the magazine may change completely. Therefore it is better not to solicit some kinds of accounts until the ultimate image of the publication is established.

* Position in Field. In general, magazines in each field are rated by agencies in numerical order according to the quantity of advertising they carry. The leading magazine is usually referred to as "top book" and spends most of its time defending itself against competitors. Since advertising commitments have not increased substantially in recent years, there has been a mad scramble in the trade field to steal dollars from other magazines. The top book normally keeps its percentage of the total advertising commitments, with the shifting of space taking place among the newer or less successful publications. Virtually every page sold in the scientific area must come out of the billings of another publication.

* Size of the Publisher or Representative. The size of the operation of a publisher or advertising representative has a great effect on advertising sales. The more publications a publisher or his representative has, the more salesmen he has calling on agencies. The better known the publisher or representative is among the agencies, the better rapport he has with agency personnel. Since much advertising is sold on friendship and personal relationships, at least at the agency level, this is important. Agencies often depend on advertising salesmen for leads on new business. Obviously, the more salesmen a publisher or representative has, the more leads he can provide.

* Trading Editorial Content for Advertising. The most effective way to get ad-

vertising is to publish editorial material for an advertiser that describes the company or its product. Such an article will often prompt the advertiser to place a certain amount of advertising in cooperative magazines. This is common practice in the business publishing field. Some controlled publications use publicity releases as their entire editorial content. These releases are keyed on reader service cards and the inquiries received through the journal are used as a lever to obtain advertising. Advertisers are well aware that the number of news releases they can have published in such magazines is directly related to the amount of advertising they place. It might also be said here that these publications may control their circulation by sending copies only to people who fill out cards. One important value of the new product section is that it provides the sales staff with an idea of what kind of items will do well in a magazine when advertised. These responses can also be followed up at a later date to determine if the product inquired about was purchased.

• Market Research. Advertisers are always hungry for information about the market for their products. Most publishers or representatives provide this information to some degree. Usually such studies pertain to the size of the market for a group or specific class of products and purport to show the relative market positions of individual advertisers as well as their percentage of the market. Such activities are expensive but essential to successful advertising sales.

• Inquiry Response. Reader service inquiries have grown to be one of the most important factors in selling product advertising to some advertisers. Strangely enough, advertisers do not normally relate inquiries to sales but evaluate the inquiries received on a quantitative basis. A large number of inquiries is a good sales tool, although sometimes too large a number makes the advertisers suspicious. Inquiries are essential to holding advertisers and are often helpful in getting new advertisers; however, they will not overcome deficiencies in the other areas described in this section. In other words, inquiries are necessary for advertising to exist but will not sell advertising entirely on their own.

• Number of New Product Releases. I have mentioned before that new product releases are helpful in determining the type of products a magazine can sell. They also provide valuable leads over which to perform surveys. Another benefit is that each time a company has a news release in a magazine, the resulting inquiries constitute a communication with the sales department of that company. Since advertising sales depend to some extent on the number and quality of contacts with advertisers, the contacts then provided are extremely helpful.

• Help from Company Officials and Friends. All advertising sales personnel, from the salesmen up to the publisher of a magazine, spend their time trying to reach people as high up the corporate executive ladder as possible. Contact at the top management level is extremely helpful in obtaining an advertising schedule. Unfortunately, few salesmen ever get to talk to people at the executive level. Contact with top executives can also be dangerous if not handled carefully, because in many cases it will alienate the people at lower levels over whose heads one must vault to reach top management. This is especially important if efforts to reach management are unsuccessful, for one is then left with no friends and several enemies.

• Editorial and Advertising Professional Readership Studies. Advertising agencies are constantly demanding proof that the editorial content and advertising in a publication are read. Because they are suspicious of any studies performed by a publication itself about the quantity of its readership, several independent services have evolved that provide this information to agencies. All agencies accept the results of such studies without question and they are immensely helpful in selling space. In some cases agencies refuse to buy advertising in publications that do not provide surveys of this kind. Ballot Research readership studies performed by Strach, Inra, Hooper Inc. are the best known and least expensive of these groups, although there are many others. The cost of a Ballot Research study of one issue is about $2000.

• Comparative Readership Studies. Comparative readership studies that prove that a magazine is read as well as or better than its competitors are extremely valuable. However, such studies will be believed by advertisers only if they are conducted by an independent objective organization such as a large advertiser or recognized professional research organization. Advertisers will not believe comparative readership studies performed by publishers.

• Inquiry Follow-Up Studies. Many publishers have developed a technique for following up the inquiries resulting from advertisements and new product releases in their magazines. These follow-up studies always prove helpful when they turn out well and usually guarantee advertising in a given product area. The most effective time for such a survey is six months to one year after an advertisement or news release appears.

Before embarking on what may be an expensive and fruitless effort to obtain advertising, the publisher must first determine whether his audience constitutes a sufficient market for enough potential advertisers to make the effort worthwhile. In making this evaluation, consumer products such as automobiles, liquor, business machines, etc. should not be considered, since very few of these advertisers use vertical or small-circulation publications. Exceptions to this are computers and calculators, which are scientific tools as well as business machines. For the most part, however, prospective advertisers will be limited to the products, services, and literature peculiar to the journal's audience. Advertising may be perceived as a service to the readership, not just excess pages to be tolerated. This is true especially in research areas that depend on advanced technology and new products, e.g., in computer technology.

Usually the services of a good consultant familiar with the scientific advertising area can be very helpful in evaluating whether a magazine has potential, who its prospects may be, and how to price the space most advantageously. The managing editor of a publication already successfully selling advertising would also be a source of sound advice. Publisher's representatives specializing in society or journal advertising sales will often offer constructive suggestions without charge.

Once the decision has been made to accept advertising, the publisher must choose whether to use an in-house sales effort or hire an outside publisher's representative. In either case, it must be remembered that it is absolutely essential for a publication to have personal contact with prospective advertisers and their agencies. Advertising cannot be sold by direct mail, although a good direct mail program is helpful in conjunction with personal sales calls. A minimum in-house staff would consist of a full-time salesman and secretarial assistant. A modest budget for such a staff, exclusive of rent and administrative overhead, would be as follows:

Salesman's salary	$35,000
Travel and entertaining expense	10,000
Phone expense	8,000
Secretarial assistant	12,000
Office supplies	6,000
Mail promotion	7,000
	$78,000

A publisher's representative, on the other hand, operates entirely on a percentage of what he sells. This varies from 20 to 30% depending on the services he is to perform. The advantage here is that no investment is required by the publisher. Some representatives will handle the entire advertising function including production, billing, promotion, collections, and selling. In selecting a representative, however, the following factors should be considered.

• Does he have a good reputation? Check with both his clients and customers. A reputable publisher's representative will provide a list of each and invite you to interview them.

• How many publications do his salesmen handle? No salesman can effectively handle more than six publications. While a firm may handle many publications, the individual salesman handling your magazine must be able to afford you sufficient contacts.

• Does he know your market? A salesman must be able to interpret effectively the market that the publication represents to the prospect's products. To do this, he must understand the products and show that they are used.

• Is the firm well known among advertising agencies?

• Is it a full-service organization with facilities to perform all functions you require of them?

• What is its sales record for its current clients? Have the advertising billings increased or decreased relative to the competition?

INTERRELATION OF EXHIBIT SPACE AND ADVERTISING

Societies that already have an exhibit connected with their annual meeting can increase the revenue from both exhibit space and journal advertising by putting the management of both in the same hands. Since, in most cases, exhibit management can be handled more cheaply and more efficiently by outside professional convention managers, the advantages of having both handled by the same firm are myriad. Because exhibitors are also the best advertising prospects for a society's journal and vice versa, each can have a synergistic effect on the other. There are several organizations that can handle exhibit sales, advertising sales, and convention management. Societies that now have these functions divided, either by the use of two different outside firms or by handling exhibit space internally and advertising externally, ought to consider the positive effect on income that will be produced by concentrating both activities in the hands of one competent group. One benefit of concentration in this way is that advertisers buying space in the publication can be offered a price "deal" on exhibit space. Likewise, exhibitors can be offered preferential advertising display rates.

CONCLUSION

In general the amount of advertising that can be sold in a journal is directly proportional to the compromises the publisher is willing to make with tradition. Undoubtedly, some historical ideas of format and presentation will have to give way to attract a significant amount of advertising.

Management should approach the problem by considering all changes that will make the journal more attractive to advertisers short of interfering with the editorial prestige and value of the journal.

Obviously the journal publisher's primary responsibility is to provide the reader with high-quality credible scientific information. It should be remembered, however, that changing the appearance of the package in which the editorial material is presented does not modify the editorial quality.

Many subscribers would prefer not to have any advertising in their journal. However, faced with a choice between advertising and no journal at all, they will, in most cases, accept the advertising. Usually subscribers will also accept the format changes necessary to attract advertisers as long as editorial quality does not suffer.

REFERENCES

1. Abelson, P.; Ormes, R. V. Supporting society journals. Science 193(4247): 9; 1976.
2. Scherago, E. J. Testimony before the Select Committee on Small Business of the United States Senate. May 24, 1976.
3. King, J. S. In a peripheral vein: an essay on parasitism. Clin. Chem. 22(7): 85A; 1976.

Page Charges

A. F. Spilhaus, Jr.

Page charges are an extremely important source of revenue for some journals. They may cover half or even more of the total cost of publication. I have heard some publishers say that page charges are the funds they collect most easily; yet I know that others find that payments are extracted only with great pain and difficulty. In any event, financing journal publication through page charges is a course fraught with uncertainty today, and publishers using this method would do well to keep their options open.

There are sound philosophical arguments in favor of the page charge and many practical advantages to it. But page charges also have many disadvantages. Funding pressures and uncertainties in federal policies related to page charges have created an anxious atmosphere. For those who are wedded to page charges, largely publishers in the physical sciences, breaking the bonds would be an exceedingly difficult task. Many are tenaciously asserting that the page charge is the only course: they are terrorized by visions of a traumatic period of change if the locus of federal subsidy for publication shifted suddenly from the producer's end of the system to the user's end.

DEVELOPMENT OF THE PAGE CHARGE

Page charges as we know them today were first adopted by the American Physical Society in 1930. The practice grew steadily after World War II. The adoption in 1961 of a federal policy that supported the page charge principle and encouraged federal agencies, contractors, and grantees to honor such page charges gave impetus to wider adoption of the practice. This policy has been reiterated and strengthened in subsequent years. The present policy can best be presented by an excerpt from a statement released by the Federal Council for Science and Technology on November 8, 1974 (Federal Register document 74–27010).

> The publication of research results in an essential part of the research process. This has been recognized in part through authorization to pay publication costs from Federal research grant and contract funds. It is the intention of the Federal Government when making research grants or contracts that costs of such publications, including page charges, should continue to be borne from the grant or contract, if other sources are not available.

Scientific policy representatives of Federal agencies that constitute the Federal Council for Science and Technology have established the following criteria for honoring page charge bills submitted by journal publishers.

(1) The research papers report work supported by the Government.

(2) Mandatory or voluntary page charge policies are acceptable, provided that the page charge policy of the publication is administered impartially for Government and non-Government sponsored research projects.

(3) The journals involved are not operated for profit.

Federal policy has encouraged an increasing dependence on page charges by not-for-profit publishers of science and engineering. A 1976 study of page charge practices performed under contract for the National Science Foundation states, "64 percent of the larger professional societies and 34 percent of the smaller societies levy charges. University presses rarely do so, and profit-making publishers never do" (1). Actually, some profit-making publishers do take advantage of page charges directly and others do so by receiving the support indirectly through a society that collects the charges and then uses the money to make payment by the society for publication of the journal.

HOW THE PAGE CHARGE WORKS

The current rates for page charges range from about $20 to over $100 per page. Practices range from a purely voluntary assessment to a strictly mandatory one. Most organizations that consider the page charge to be voluntary make it quite clear that payment of the charge is not a prerequisite to publication: they do so by not seeking information, before final acceptance of the paper, about the author's intention to pay. It is the policy of the American Geophysical Union never to inform selection editors of who has and who has not honored the charges.

Many shades of gray exist between the voluntary and mandatory page charge. Most of these build upon the basic voluntary charge with various methods and degrees of coercion to encourage payment. The two-track approach is one of the most widely used methods. Papers for which the page charge will not be honored are put in a queue that is published more slowly than those for which the charge is honored. This can be a financially convenient trick because the number of unpaid pages can with ease be accurately regulated by allowing the delay time to float. In theory, as the delay time gets long, those who cannot pay will reduce their submissions, so an equilibrium should be reached quickly if authors can be kept aware of the delays. In practice, however, it may be difficult to attract back authors who have been turned away by long delays.

If the page charge is not honored, reprints may be withheld or charged for at very high rates. An enforcement program can include asking federal grantors to remind grantees of their responsibilities or, at a lower level, trying to bring the forces of peer pressure and conscience to bear on reluctant authors and their institutions.

VARIATIONS ON THE THEME

I suspect that hidden page charges are nearly as common as explicit ones. Thus far I have discussed only simple per page assessments by a publisher to an author, but many variations on the theme achieve the same result: subsidy of publication by the author, which must be considered in the same class as page charges. Charges for reprints, plates, color figures, excess pagination, composition, and article submission are examples of these subsidies. They are used by publishers both alone and in combination with the explicit page charge to provide income at the input end of the system.

Reprint charges have proved an effective supplement or substitute for explicit page charges in the past, but the widespread use of photocopying seems to have somewhat reduced the demand for reprints and their future as a major income source is uncertain. Reprints have been used in combination with the page charge in that frequently a fixed number are provided gratis if the page charge is honored with additional reprints available at or near production costs, or, if more profit is desired, at some multiple of cost, which can be as high as five. One simple variation is the substitution of a substantial flat per page rate for reprints that becomes in essence a page charge; this option has also been used to introduce the page charge to book publication.

A charge applied to all articles submitted is justified on the basis that the expense of selecting the worthy should be borne by all manuscripts that go through the system. Actually, in most cases, rejected manuscripts take more time and expense than accepted ones, and therefore one could justifiably apply the submission charge against the page charge bill if the article is accepted. A simple way to do this is to make the first page free.

PROS AND CONS

The use of page charges has been furiously debated on practical, theoretical, and moral grounds. Federal policies support the page charge mechanism but one of the practical arguments against page charges is that these policies appear at present to be fluid and can so easily change. Arguments in favor of page charges rest on the presumption that wide dissemination of scientific results to individuals is of benefit to the entire society. If publishers of low-circulation journals were prepared virtually to abandon dissemination to individuals, they might, judging by the financial success of many commercially published journals designed for institutional sale, survive without the page charge.

Since nonprofit publishers, the principal users of page charges, are attempting first to serve the best interest of society as a whole rather than to make a profit for stockholders or individuals, it is incumbent on them to examine the problem of how to maximize the net benefit to society resulting from their journals. The question is, at what circulation is the benefit maximized?

Before further discussion some common terminology should be established, as well as a broad grasp of the relationship of production costs to number of pages and number of copies printed. Publication production costs are divided into four categories. 1) Fixed costs are those that are relatively independent of the number of pages or copies printed. These include the costs for selection editors and for many overhead items. 2) Page costs are those that vary directly with the number of pages but are independent of the number of copies printed such as composition and press-room and bindery setups. 3) Copy costs vary only with the number of copies. These are usually minimal for short-run scientific journals; they include subscription maintenance and the per copy costs for handling and mailing. 4) Impression costs vary with both the number of copies and the number of pages. One can simplify this breakdown by classifying fixed costs and page costs as "first-copy" costs: the cost that would be incurred even if only one copy were edited, produced, and distributed. Copy costs and impression costs make up what an economist would call the marginal costs, that is, the cost of running off an additional copy once all the costs of publishing at least one copy have been paid.

Now to return to the question, at what circulation is the benefit to society maximized? In the Report of the Task Group on the Economics of Primary Publication of the Committee on Scientific and Technical Communication of the National Academy of Sciences (2), it is argued that the total amount of money that enlightened buyers are willing to allocate to the purchase of a journal represents the gross value of this journal to society. If we consider an infinitely variable price, we find that as price decreases the number of buyers increases and the gross value increases by the increase in number of buyers times the price at that level. However, we are trying to maximize net value, and for copies that are provided at less than the cost of printing and mailing that additional copy, there is a reduction rather than an increase in the net value. Thus we find that the maximum net benefit to society is achieved if copies can be distributed for prices as low as, but not lower than, the marginal copy cost. If all costs incurred through the production of the first copy were subsidized by a page charge, all copies could be sold at this marginal cost. The Task Group reached the conclusion that:

> When the prices buyers are willing to pay reflect correct judgments of the value of journals and if the existence and properties of journals are assumed independent of pricing policy, the progress of science and technology is optimized by a policy that sets the price to buyers at the run-off cost and supports prerun cost in some other way.

In support of page charges, it is also argued that publication is part of the research process. Indeed for science, publication is both the input and the output: for individual researchers it is an indispensable ingredient. Scientific research begins with an assimilation of previous work from the literature and is not complete until it culminates in an addition to the literature. Therefore publication is a legitimate charge to research funds. One can agree with this reasoning, but without resort to the social value arguments, one can still question whether it is necessary for the subsidy to come through the author as producer of the information. Some say that the same funds from the same pocket might be used for purchasing the information, but they ignore the value of broad dissemination. It is far simpler to reach each author at the time of publication than to reach each reader when he needs the results.

Also telling are arguments that publication benefits the author and so he should share some of the costs. In this regard page charges are analogous to paid advertising. Additionally, page charges permit a publisher to disregard to some extent the fads in research and focus on the long-term interests of the science.

Although one may believe that today most of the philosophical arguments are relatively weak, the maximization of the net value to society is not a weak argument; it is of overwhelming importance and goes to the heart of the purpose of scientific societies. For journals to give up page charges may be to give up some of their raison d'etre.

On the practical side, page charges at present represent a relatively easily collected source of money, especially for journals publishing work by scientists in government agencies. Support of first-copy costs by page charges has the additional advantage of introducing considerable flexibility into a journal's budget. For the budget of a short-run journal, a significant fraction of the total cost is first-copy; if this is covered by the page charges, fluctuations in the number of pages printed in a volume can be absorbed much more easily. Table 1 shows the effect on the subscription rate required to break even with page charges at various levels. It is easily seen that the smaller the circulation the more significant the page charge can be to the financing mix of a journal. Rarely does the page charge cover the full first-copy cost, but as it increases to that level, the subscription rate required to break even varies far less as the circulation changes.

In publications issued by societies, it is common to sustain differential pricing through which the member receives journals at a rate near the production costs and libraries pay from 2 to 10 times more to make up the difference between actual page charge collections and the first-copy costs. Without page charges, differentials may be so great that they will be hard to maintain practically or individual rates will become so high as to be unattractive.

A word of caution on the practice of differential pricing: it irritates librarians; they call it discriminatory and some are claiming it is illegal. Unfortunately publishers have not made clear how to evaluate their products so that the librarian can recognize the terrific information bargain that results from page charge support (see chapt. 1).

The philosophical arguments against the page charge are dependent on the degree of indifference to dissemination to individuals. Without agreement that the first priority is to maximize the net benefit to society and that broad dissemination maximizes benefit, the arguments favoring page charges break down. And from the pragmatic viewpoint, there are some real disadvantages related to page charges.

The page charge encourages lengthy publication. Some authors say "I'm going

TABLE 1. Subscription rates required to break even for a 6500-page journal with various page charge levels and numbers of subscribers

Number of Subscribers	Page Charge			
	$117	$80	$40	$0
1000	$52	$293	$553	$813
4000	52	112	178	243
8000	52	83	115	145

to pay for it. Why do I have to cut it down?'' The editor and publisher have less incentive to force the reduction of printed pages as long as they know each page will be paid for. Giving in to such pressure from authors is a disservice to all present and future users of the literature.

A variety of problems are associated with the fact that some journals have page charges and others do not. The author's decision about which journal to choose for his paper may become an economic rather than a scientific one, thus diluting the value of the literature by diffusion of material to less appropriate outlets.

Even when page charges are truly voluntary, a certain discrimination exists against papers from authors who cannot pay. On the one hand, non-U.S. authors do not pay as frequently as U.S. authors and editors know at least this much from their correspondence with these authors. On the other hand, authors who cannot pay may be reluctant on principle to submit to a journal that assesses page charges even if the charge is voluntary. The result may be a loss of excellent papers to journals that do not have page charges. For the society publisher, this means that good papers go into competing commercial journals. The commercial journal is strengthened and the result is a reduction in the subscription dollars available for the society journal because such a large fraction of these dollars is taken by the significantly higher priced commercial counterparts. Faced with reduced resources, librarians may then turn to procuring journals through individuals, thus evading the institutional rate and further weakening the base of support for the society publications.

Another difficulty with page charges is that frequently a grantee's support will have expired before his publication finally appears in print. Money must be reserved if page charges are to be paid. Another problem is that the page charge is common in the physical sciences, less so in the life sciences, rare in engineering, and almost non-existent in the social sciences. This means that a journal spanning these general areas may have difficulty implementing page charges because some authors will not be accustomed to seeking funds for publication and will have many alternative outlets that do not charge and in some instances may pay for contributions.

A journal heavily dependent on page charges may be in a precarious position. For example, several societies assessing page charges found themselves in conflict with the U.S. Postal Service in the autumn of 1976. At that time the Postal Service attempted to make the case that payment of page charges constituted valuable consideration for publication of articles and that such articles must be considered paid advertising and be so marked and have postage paid for them at the advertising rate. At present this issue seems to have resolved itself. The Post Office has agreed that voluntary page charges (without defining voluntary) do not constitute consideration for publication, and it has proposed revised regulations that exclude scientific articles from the material that would be charged at the advertising postage rate. Such articles are, however, subject to the above labeling requirement (but not additional postal charges) should they be paid for by mandatory page charges. I expect that there will be pressure from several societies to have this labeling requirement modified by congressional action. A possible concern is that the Internal Revenue Service could, by logic parallel to that used by the Postal Service, try to tax page charge revenues as advertising income.

PROGNOSIS FOR THE FUTURE

For the future we should recognize that the page charge concept is not restricted to ink-on-paper formats. We may have to change the name, but subsidy at the author's end can provide similar benefits in the electronic era. One of the most important future considerations will be copyright. It appears that there will be some form of compensation for photocopying. However, this compensation will only apply to material that is copyrighted. It may not be possible to copyright the works of government employees, and we are hearing rumbles that certain industries are going to be unwilling to transfer copyright. It therefore seems that it will be more than reasonable for publishers to assess a kind of prelicensing fee from these individuals, perhaps in the form of a page charge. In the future some publishers may waive the page charge only if the full copyright privileges are transferred. With the growing intrusion of wholesalers, such as the National Technical Information Service, who bear no responsibility for the quality of their wares, it is necessary that responsible publishers protect themselves and their immediate users. Using page charges to keep subscription rates down and therefore to enhance individual accessibility is an important alternative to consider.

This chapter presents some of the bases on which a decision of whether and how to use page charges should be made. It is essential for the not-for-profit publisher to maintain a very flexible stance with regard to his funding opportunities at this time. The practice of the American Geophysical Union reflects this philosophy. It usually uses voluntary page charges; the two-track system exists for several journals; some journals have no page charges; and for some items, mandatory page charges are imposed. In some cases, high-cost reprints substitute for page charges. The particular mix suitable for one audience may not work with another. One must experiment cautiously and seek the most competitive position that is consistent with the publishing objectives of one's organization.

REFERENCES

1. Hardman, M. Federal support of scientific and technical publication. Report to the National Science Foundation under Contract No. C–1001; 1976; NTIS PB 265–543.
2. Herring, C.; Katz, D. L.; Linder, C. H.; Luntz, J. D.; Weyl, F. J. Report of the task group on the economics of primary publication. Washington, DC: National Academy of Sciences; 1970; NTIS PB 194–400.

Journal Income: A Multipublisher's View

R. H. Marks

The income to support a scientific journal comes from a variety of sources including publication charges, nonmember subscriptions, member subscriptions, royalties, article reprints, back numbers, microfilm, and advertising sales.

The basic elements of scientific journal income are shown in Fig. 1 for six journals of the American Institute of Physics (AIP). The largest income source is nonmember subscriptions, which account for 50% of the total. This is closely followed by publication charges, which provide for 38%. Member subscriptions bring in 6%, and all other income sources make up the remaining 6%.

SUBSCRIPTION INCOME

The total subscription income collected over a 10-year period, starting in 1971, for the AIP and member society journals is shown in Fig. 2. In 1971 the total subscription income (member and nonmember) for AIP journals was about $2.1 million. Subscriptions to AIP member society journals added another $1.5 million, bringing the total to slightly over $3.6 million. By 1980 total subscription income had risen to $9.9 million, with AIP journals accounting for $5.1 million and the member society journals the other $4.8 million.

In 1971 the AIP and its member societies published 70,000 text pages and sold 1450 advertising pages. By 1980 the number of text pages had increased to 86,000. At the same time, the number of advertising pages dropped to 1365. The AIP in 1971 also published the English translation of 26,500 pages from 14 Soviet journals. For 1980 the Soviet translation program included a total of 19 journals and the number of Soviet pages had increased to 36,000.

Some of the increase in subscription revenue was also required to cover inflationary increases in the cost of printing, paper, and mailing. These increases in cost were partially compensated for by the use of more efficient web-offset press equipment and the increased availability of high-quality, lightweight paper. The introduction of the computer for automated subscription fulfillment and mailing label production also helped to lower costs by improving productivity of a labor-intensive operation. Automatic wrapping and labeling equipment produced further economies, but these unfortunately were more than negated by increases in the cost of

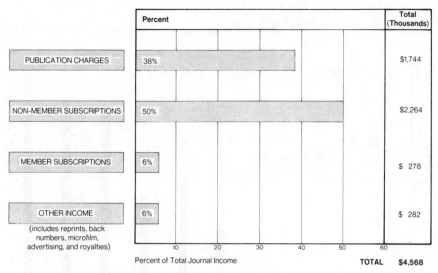

Fig. 1. Basic elements of scientific journal income for six AIP journals are shown in percentage and in total dollars for 1980.

postage. The use of plastic shrink wrap has dramatically reduced claims for replacement of lost or damaged issues.

PUBLICATION CHARGES

Publication charge income (1–3), i.e., income from page charges, collected over the same period is shown in Fig. 3. Starting at a total of just over $3.5 million in 1971, this income reached a peak of more than $4.3 million in 1979. In 1980 income dipped to $3.8 million. The AIP journals received just over $1.7 million (46%), and the member society journals accounted for the remaining $2.1 million (54%). This record is remarkable considering that the publication charge is not mandatory. Editorial acceptance of articles is unaffected by payment or nonpayment. Nearly all institutions, companies, and government agencies supporting physics research have accepted the moral obligation of making the payment.

Despite inflation, today's publication charge rates are only about 18% higher than they were in 1970. The most dramatic cost reduction was made in composition expense. The switch from Monotype to typewriter composition on a larger page (4) reduced this component by $15–$20 per page. The recent introduction of computer photocomposition has also helped to control composition expense by further improving productivity over typewriter composition. The line was held on editorial mechanics cost by upgrading staff and streamlining operation procedures. The switch from letterpress to offset printing made it possible to eliminate the use of expensive illustration engravings. Engraving cost (5), which ran about $5 per page, was

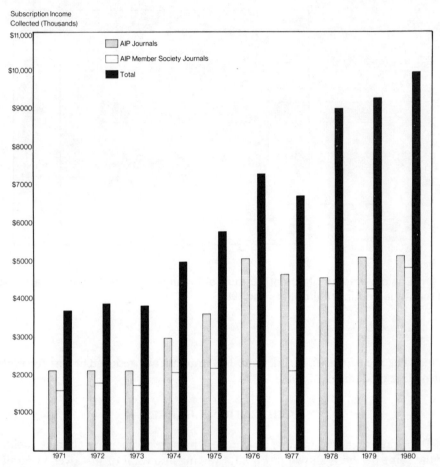

Fig. 2.   Total subscription income collected over a 10-year period starting in 1971.
The increase covered a growth in the number of pages published from 70,000 in 1971
to 86,000 in 1980. Over the same period, the number of Soviet journal pages translated went from 26,500 to 36,000.

reduced to less than $1.50 per page by using an in-house camera to produce interme-
diate illustration prints that are pasted directly on the composed page.

SUBSCRIPTION RATES

The effect of publication charge income on journal price and circulation can be
seen by comparing AIP archival journals with the AIP Soviet translation journals.
The translation journals share the same income sources except that they do not receive any publication charge income. The resulting subscription price for the Soviet
translation journals averages about 17.8 cents per translated English page. The average number of subscriptions, mainly from libraries, is about 635.

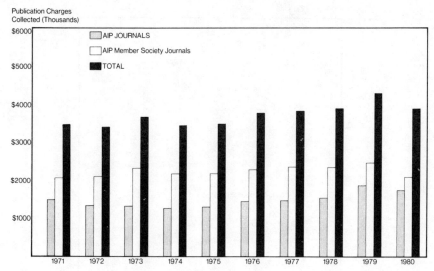

Fig. 3.   Publication charge income, collected over a 10-year period starting in 1971, reached a peak of over 4.3 million in 1979.

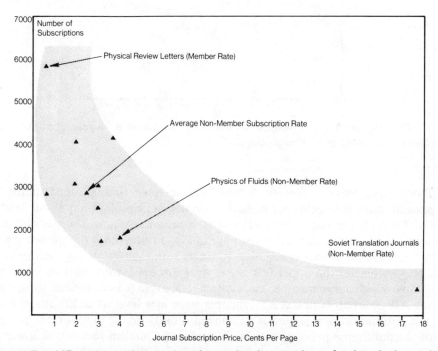

Fig. 4.   For AIP and member society journals, the number of subscriptions plotted against price per page for 1980 falls within the shaded area.

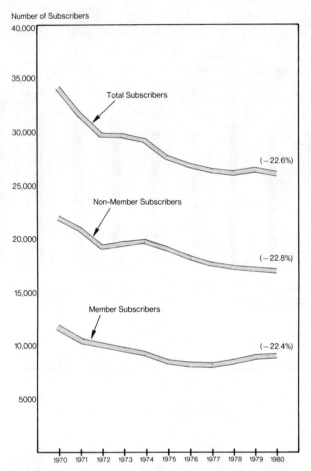

Number of Subscribers

Fig. 5.   Overall decrease in number of subscriptions over a 10-year span for the six AIP archival journals is in the range of 22.4–22.8%.

By contrast, *Physical Review Letters* has a member circulation of almost 5800 at a price of about 0.65 cents per page. Its nonmember circulation is about 2850 at a price of 3.0 cents per page. For AIP and member society journals, the number of subscriptions plotted against price per page in Fig. 4 falls within the shaded area. At the far right are the Soviet translation journals with their relatively high price and small circulation. At the upper left is *Phsyical Review Letters* with its lower price and comparatively large member circulation. The average nonmember subscription rate for AIP journals is about 2.5 cents per page at a level of 2850 subscriptions.

The publication charge plan is a financial subsidy on the input or pre–press run side of the publishing process, making it possible to publish journals at lower subscription rates and achieve a much larger circulation than journals published without the benefit of this subsidy (6).

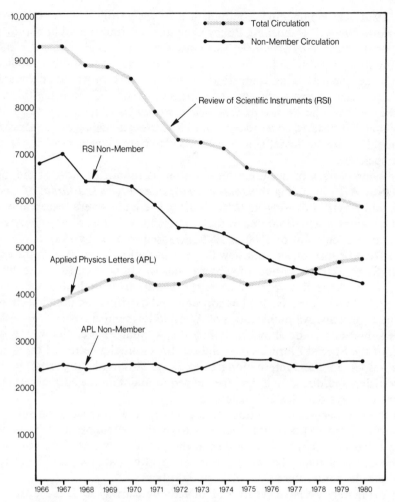

Fig. 6. Circulation over the period from 1966 to 1980 shows a substantial drop for RSI compared with a slight increase for APL.

JOURNAL CIRCULATION

Over the past 10 years, the number of subscriptions to many printed journals has been steadily declining. Figure 5 shows the decline from 1970 to 1980 for the six AIP archival journals. The decrease in journal subscriptions has been accompanied by an increase in the number of pages published. It has also coincided with the growth of computerized bibliographic search services and increased photocopying of journal articles.

The circulation picture over a 15-year span for the *Review of Scientific Instruments* is shown in Fig. 6. Total circulation in 1966 of about 9300 had decreased to

5900 by 1980. The nonmember component decreased from 6800 to 4200 over the same period. The AIP Publishing Policy Committee formed an ad hoc study group to examine the *Review of Scientific Instruments* in some detail. The scope and content of the articles published were analyzed and compared with other publications that might be considered as competition. Their conclusion was that the editorial quality was excellent and a cut above competing journals. Supporting this conclusion is the fact that the *Review of Scientific Instruments* is one of the few scientific journals that is translated cover to cover into the Russian language. The Russian edition is published by the Soviet Union under its copyright agreement with AIP and its member societies.

The same pattern of declining subscriptions is found for most of the journals published by AIP, including the *Journal of Applied Physics, Journal of Chemical Physics*, and *Physical Review A, B, C*, and *D*. There are several exceptions to this trend of declining circulation; one of these, also shown in Fig. 6, is *Applied Physics Letters*. Total circulation of 3700 in 1966 increased to 4700 by 1981.

In 1976 AIP introduced four new Soviet translation journals with the expectation that the break-even number of subscriptions would be reached by the third year of publication. After five years, none of these journals is in the black.

The AIP Marketing Division has concentrated its efforts on building circulation for the new journals. All publications of AIP and its member societies are exhibited at professional and trade shows including the Annual Physics Show, the Annual Meeting of the Special Libraries Association, the Annual Meeting of the American Library Association, and international book fairs. This marketing program, including advertising and direct mail, has also helped to maintain the current level of subscriptions to our older established journals.

As the number of subscriptions to a given journal decreases, its subscription price must be increased each year, not only to offset the loss of subscription income but also to cover inflationary increases in the production cost. Some of the additional income needed may be derived from the royalties paid for photocopying of individual articles under the new U.S. copyright law.

Unfortunately we have yet to find an economical way to select, produce, and deliver only those specific articles that an individual user is interested in. Most users cannot really define what they want until they have browsed through an entire issue. During 1981 AIP serviced about 86,000 nonmember subscriptions to 63 journals. At these subscription levels, the printed journal is still by far the most economical way to distribute large amounts of information to large numbers of users at widely scattered locations.

REFERENCES

1. Barton, H. A. The publication charge plan in physics journals. Phys. Today 16:45–57; 1963.
2. Marks, R. H. Publication charge plan provides wide circulation at lower journal subscription rates. 3rd IEEE Conf. Sci. J. May 2–4, 1977; Reston, VA.
3. Capital System Group, Inc. Page-charge policies and practices in scientific and technical

publishing: a historical summary and annotated bibliography. National Science Foundation; 1976; PB 256–409.

4. Marks, R. H.; Metzner, A.W.K. Typewriter composition cuts journal costs, speeds publication. IEEE Trans. Prof. Commun. PC–16:73–79, 174; 1973.
5. Koch, M. An in-house camera system for making line and halftone illustration prints. IEEE Trans. Prof. Commun. PC–18:288; 1975.
6. Koch, H. W. Economics of primary journals in physics. Am. Assoc. Adv. Sci. meeting. December 29, 1969; Boston, MA; NTIS PB 190–490.

Editorial Operations

Lewis I. Gidez

The nature of the editorial function in scientific publications has never really been completely defined. The role of an editor, and consequently the elements of expense in editorial operation, depend on the editorial hierarchy, which in turn may be a function of many factors: the scope of the journal, whether the journal is a society publication, the number of pages to be printed each year, the policies concerning the peer review process, and the general philosophy of what constitutes a publishable scientific article. The bottom line from the point of view of the scientific community is the published article. Thus an editor is accountable to the scientific community: to readers (not just subscribers) and to authors of all papers, accepted or not, submitted to the journal. Objective measures of success of a journal are the rate of manuscript submission, how a journal fares in a citation analysis, and the frequency at which current or older issues are signed out of libraries. This last criterion is especially important when library budgets are limited, and decisions regarding subscription renewals are made on the basis of journal use. From the point of view of management, the bottom line is hopefully a black dollar sign. Thus the editor is also accountable to the owner of the journal, whether an individual, a corporation, or a society.

Much that is covered in this chapter unavoidably overlaps other areas of income or expense. No two journals function editorially in the same fashion, and each journal is unique, reflecting the personalities, sensitivities, and professional and scientific experiences of the editors. This chapter centers primarily on expenses associated with manuscript management and tracking, the review process, scientific editing, different ways of analyzing costs, compilation and analysis of useful editorial information, and a variety of other topics well known to the scientific editor. The discussion deals with the traditional roles of author, editor, reviewer, publisher, and printer and is not concerned with such topics as editorial processing centers and camera-ready copy. In general, analyses of elements of income and elements of expense are concerned with systems, techniques, and procedures and the more impersonal aspects of scientific publication. Editors are also concerned with the same systems and procedures, but they deal primarily with people: people whose professional careers in large part are influenced by their success in publishing articles and people who pass judgment on authors, namely reviewers and associate editors. The point of view is that of a scientist–executive editor of a relatively small (1200–1500 pages per year), highly specialized nonsociety journal with 2000–2300 subscribers.

Some types of editorial costs are standard regardless of the size of the journal. These have to do with the tools of the editorial office and are not treated in depth. Needless to say the initial costs of a journal editorial office can be appreciable when one considers the expense of office furniture, typewriters, postage meters, copy machines, etc. Other types of costs are less tangible and visible but are more important in maintaining the equilibrium between the pressures of quality, with its attendant potentially high costs, and the pressures of fixed economy and attendant lower costs and quality.

The editorial structure and review procedures can have tremendous impact on both tangible and intangible costs of a journal; tangible, in the sense that the annual bottom-line profit or loss is a function of the editorial process; intangible, in the sense that over a period of years a journal's fortunes, scientific and financial, are subtly affected by editorial policy in ways that may not easily be documented.

PERSONNEL

A critical determinant of editorial expense is the editorial structure of the journal. It is necessary to delineate the responsibilities of editors at various levels, whatever their titles may be. Of special importance are the job descriptions of the editor or editors who have the primary editorial and/or administrative roles. These individuals should know what their expected roles are so there are no surprises, no duplication of effort on the one hand or complete absence of effort on the other. This may be of special significance when there is a complete change in journal management or when there is a partial change, with a new editor joining a managing editor or executive editor in the overall management of editorial operations.

The question is often raised, should editors be paid for their services? Here we must differentiate between, on the one hand, the editor whose primary role is securing scientific articles and assuming prime responsibility for the review of manuscripts and the decision to accept or reject and, on the other hand, the managing or executive or assistant editor whose main functions are administrative and managerial and who is the liaison between editor and printer, or editor and author, or editor and reviewer. The former type of editor is sometimes categorized as an amateur editor in that he or she is not professionally trained as an editor, but rather is a distinguished scientist who probably has had some experience as a reviewer or associate editor; his prestige and reputation in the scientific community will hopefully ensure a constant flow of manuscripts and a fair evaluation. By tradition, this type of editor is not paid a salary, although he may receive his expenses and either no honorarium or only a modest one. "Modest" may mean a token payment of a few hundred dollars or many thousand dollars a year in *supplemental* compensation. In general, research funds are harder and harder to come by, because relatively less money is available and competition is more keen for the amount that is available. Because publication is vital for continuing support and promotion, and because the scientific literature is growing as a result of expansion of existing journals and publication of new journals, it is more and more difficult to convince scientists to become editors; they may be enticed only by an honorarium and/or the backup of an ongoing editorial operation.

The main compensation of an editor usually comes from the institution at which he is domiciled or from grants. Editors may often underestimate the amount of time they feel they must spend on journal activities and consequently after they have been on the job may seek additional compensation. Certainly, editors cannot expect a granting agency or an academic institution to pay for a disproportionate amount of nonresearch and/or nonacademic activities, and certainly granting agencies would not tolerate such a situation. Remuneration of an editor can be a significant item of expense, even if only on an ad hoc basis. Financial arrangements should be clearly delineated in advance.

The managing or executive editor is different. This type of editor is the so-called professional editor and is paid a competitive salary by the journal or sponsoring society. He or she may be full time or part time, depending on the job description and the size and scope of the journal. It is beyond the purview of this chapter to outline duties of a managing or executive or assistant editor. Such an individual may or may not have a scientific background, although a scientist in this position may be an asset to a journal's operation.

Secretarial services are a major expense. The number of hours a secretary or editorial assistant must work to maintain an efficient editorial operation is directly proportional to the number of manuscripts submitted. Each submitted manuscript (original or revised) may require a total of 1.5–2.5 hours of an editorial assistant's time for routine management; logging in, filing, acknowledgments, miscellaneous record keeping, forwarding to editors or reviewers. Perhaps 60% of an editorial assistant's time is spent on such routine manuscript handling. With 180–200 new manuscripts a year, and with 85–105 papers published each year, 18–24 hours per week of secretarial assistance may be adequate. The total expense of secretarial services may also depend on the editorial structure of the journal. A system in which a manuscript is sent directly from the editorial office to a reviewer who then returns it to the editor will be less costly than one that has a more involved review process and consequently would occupy more secretarial time. Some journals provide part-time assistants for associate editors or members of editorial boards. For many journals whose editorial structure is more or less centralized, secretaries employed by the institution or society may perform their services on behalf of the journal at no direct expense to the journal. The time involved is usually small in comparison with other duties. However, the aggregate number of hours may be appreciable, and if the cost for them was evaluated it could increase secretarial expenses by 30–50%.

From a journal's point of view a full-time editorial assistant may not be necessary; from an author's point of view an editorial office should be occupied 35 hours a week. Perhaps the most inconvenient aspect of not having 35 hours of help per week is that the telephone is not always covered. This can be rectified with a telephone answering device that can record a message or by having an alternate phone number that is always covered, such as in the editor's laboratory. Both situations are satisfactory and which one is adopted depends on an editor's style of working. Whatever solution is applied, it is absolutely essential that authors have reasonably easy access to an editor.

POSTAGE EXPENSES

Postage costs for manuscript management and the review process may be substantial, and these costs will vary according to the policies of the journal and the depth of the review process. At one extreme, prestamped (or premetered), preaddressed envelopes may be provided to all who are involved in reviewing and evaluating manuscripts. This is a greatly appreciated convenience for the reviewer; he or she need not be concerned with how much postage is needed or who will pay for it. Such a courtesy is little enough compensation for the reviewer who spends many hours with the manuscript. At the other extreme, return postage is not prepaid, and reviewers (or their institutions) must assume the postal expenses. All else being equal, the latter journal would spend about half as much on manuscript postage as the first journal, and manuscripts could be processed somewhat more rapidly. This may be desirable for saving money, but such a policy could be a deterrent to an efficient review process.

A third option may be the best solution for saving postage expenses and time in the editorial office without inconveniencing the referees. The reviewer is instructed to keep the manuscript for one year in the event that a revision is returned for rereview. At the end of the year the manuscript is then destroyed. Thus all the reviewer has to do is return his evaluation to the editorial office (in a stamped, preaddressed envelope) and safely file the manuscript. Of course reviewers are reminded that the manuscripts are confidential and are to be used for no other purpose than their evaluation.

Editorial offices handle a considerable amount of nonmanuscript mail, but certainly most of the postage is used for manuscript routing. Postage expenses may amount to 10-25% of the total operating expense of an editorial office (excluding personnel). For the *Journal of Lipid Research* the mean percentage over an eight-year period (1973-1980) was 19.5 ± 5.5, with a range of 8-24%. For a larger journal with five times more papers submitted, postage expenses averaged 20.5% of editorial expenses based on data for 1972, 1973, 1976, and 1977. The cost for the *Journal of Lipid Research* has averaged almost $10 per manuscript over an eight-year period; for the larger journal just mentioned, postage costs were $8-11 per manuscript. For yet another large journal with approximately 1250 submissions per year, postage expenses in 1980 were about $9.30 per manuscript. In evaluating postal expenses, one must consider increases in postal rates (6 cents in the early 1970's to 20 cents in late 1981 for first-class letters), as well as significant changes in manuscript submission rate. However, for budgetary purposes, a figure of $10-15 per manuscript could be used for most journals (less if the manuscripts were retained by the reviewers as described above), and this would include ancillary postal expenses.

MANUSCRIPT MANAGEMENT AND THE REVIEW PROCESS

Total publication time can be conveniently divided into three segments: the review, the revision, and the production. The first period is from the date of receipt to the initial decision. This time period applies to all manuscripts and is a measure of the speed and efficiency of the manuscript management and review process. It is usually independent of the authors unless the submitted manuscript is incomplete. From the point of view of most authors and editors, this is probably the rate-limiting period in the overall "production" of a journal article. What occurs in this period may have more to do with a journal's image and prestige than any other facet of the publication process.

The review process is a critical factor in the success of a journal and the impression that journal makes in the scientific community. Perhaps the most common grievance of an author concerns the inordinate length of the review process when he or she must wait occasionally several months for a decision. An author whose paper has undergone a prolonged review process, irrespective of whether the review is favorable or negative, may think twice about submitting other articles to that journal. The net effect over a period of time may be the lessening of the journal's prestige because it will not attract new, exciting, and important papers. Therefore it is incumbent on editors to be constantly aware of how much time the review process consumes and to take appropriate steps when there are inexcusable delays or when the mean review time becomes progressively longer. If the overall review process is too extensive (e.g., several layers of referees and editors), it must be made less complicated, but without too much relinquishment of the depth and quality of the review.

The referee's commitment to evaluate a manuscript thoroughly and promptly is a critical component of the review process; reviewers must be chosen carefully on the basis of their scientific expertise and their efficiency. An individual who agreed via a prior telephone call to be a referee is more apt to be prompt than the unsolicited individual who receives a manuscript. However, in using the telephone to contact reviewers one has to consider the economic impact of increased phone use, whether via a WATS line or via standard direct dialing. There is more to the review process than getting referees to be prompt. Poor reviews, no matter how rapid, are of no use to the author or editor, and they may result in additional expense and delays when a more adequate evaluation is sought. The review process is concerned primarily with the scientific merits of a manuscript. The constructive critiques of referees and editor usually contain adequate directions and suggestions on the scientific substance of the paper for the authors to prepare an acceptable revised version. At the same time editors must instruct authors to rewrite where necessary when poor syntax, an abundance of misspelled words, and punctuation errors make a manuscript difficult to read. When the manuscript is returned for revision, the editor should remind the authors to be certain about correct labeling and placement of figures and tables, correct citations and references, and accurate listing of data in tables. Editors are responsible for insisting on careful preparation of manuscripts by authors beyond the normal instructions and guidelines.

In 1979 the *Journal of Lipid Research* instituted two major changes in editorial policy in order to decrease both the review time and total time for publication. These changes were phased in gradually over a six-month period. By eliminating one level in a three-tier review system and by telephoning all reviewers in advance, the mean decision time was shortened by 2.5 weeks. Equally important, the standard deviation of the mean (a reflection of the range of decision times) was cut in half; the very long review period was virtually eliminated. The second change was to ease restrictions on the size of individual issues. This resulted in larger issues, with some articles being published one month sooner than they would have been in prior years. Authors were pleased by the net result. Moreover the manuscript submission rate increased 22% over a rate that had been fairly steady over a nine-year period, and this increased rate has held for nearly two years.

The price of these changes was substantial. Personnel and production expenses were increased, and telephone expenses quadrupled. This anecdotal material is included to stress an important question that any editor or society must raise when costly editorial policies are instituted. Will the changes be cost-effective? Journals must show a net profit to allow for growth, inflation, and fiscal emergencies.

The second segment of publication time is the time for revision of a potentially acceptable manuscript. Editors have little control over what happens during this period other than to inquire about seemingly long delays in receipt of a revision. Editors may choose to ignore this period; nevertheless they should know how much time the average author takes to revise a paper. This information, along with the manuscript submission and acceptance rates, may be important in planning the size of future issues or in decisions about expanding (or contracting) frequency of publication. Thus the revision period does have subtle economic implications, especially for the smaller journal. A survey of manuscripts accepted by the *Journal of Lipid Research* over a 3.5-year period revealed that the 10th, 50th, and 90th percentile revision times were 24 days, 57 days, and 180 days, respectively. Fifty percent of acceptable revisions were received within 57 days of the initial decision letter and 50% between 58 and 280 days. This skewed distribution to the right is due primarily to manuscripts that require rerevision and/or additional experimental work.

The third period spans the time from receipt of an accepted revision to publication. The major tasks in this segment are an evaluation of the revised manuscript, redaction, composition, printing, binding, and distribution. Each task must be completed within a well-defined period of time, because delays at any stage may result in added expense and/or late distribution. Editors must also adhere to time guidelines in submitting accepted manuscripts to the copy editor. They must be careful not to risk upsetting subsequent production sequences by extending the closing date of an issue in order to publish an extra paper or two. This may be especially applicable to the smaller journal without a policy of publishing a fixed number of pages per issue. Turnaround time for proof correction by authors must be kept at a minimum in order not to delay publication. Someone must assume responsibility for contacting tardy authors. In the absence of an author-corrected proof, total turnaround time can be held down by having the copy editor return duplicate corrected proofs to the printer and gamble that the authors would not have made substantive changes. This latter procedure may be necessary occasionally for papers from abroad.

PRODUCTION EXPENSES

Perhaps the largest single expense item is the cost of printing the journal and this is, of course, directly related to the number of pages printed. This cost may be about 35–50% of the *total* operating expenses of a journal with an additional 3–5% for mailing and storage. Here again, editorial practice determines the actual expenses. If it has a low rate of submitted manuscripts and/or a low acceptance rate, a journal can publish all accepted papers in a reasonable time. Indeed, if the rate-limiting process in the production sequence is the acceptance of papers, thin issues will result. This ususally means a profit in a given year, but even one small volume may have an adverse effect on subscription renewals. A more serious fiscal problem can result when budgets dictate that the number of pages published be kept within narrow limits. What can an editor do if the number of papers ready to be published in a given issue or two issues exceeds the available budgeted space?

1) Decrease total production costs. This subject is covered elsewhere in this book.

2) Decrease the number of pages required by changes in format and design. For example, smaller type may be used throughout the manuscript or for certain sections, such as references or methods.

3) Increase the lead time of publication, i.e. the interval between acceptance and publication. This is a stop-gap measure that is practical for only a short time. If carried on for too long, authors might revolt, especially when they see a small issue that might have contained their article.

4) Adhere to strict editorial standards in evaluating papers to curb growth. Editors may have to reexamine priorities to make certain that a manuscript reports information that is original, adequately documented, obtained by valid experimentation, and important. They may have to institute a "not for us" category. They may have to look more carefully at marginal reports and not ask for additional experimentation, which is almost an assurance of eventual acceptance. Particular care must be taken not to set up a double standard in the sense of accepting in January, when there is adequate space for May publication, a paper that would be rejected in June, when the September and November issues are rapidly filling up.

5) Increase the number of issues to be published in a year. This not only would be a major policy change but would entail considerable added expense. Superimposed on the additional cost of the extra printed pages would be increased cost of covers, binding, and mailing. These expenses would, it is hoped, be more than offset by an increase in subscription income generated by an obligatory higher subscription price and by increased reprint sales. Obviously any decision to publish extra issues would be made only with short-term assurance of a *continuous* supply of publishable manuscripts. The biggest danger is that in four or six months there would be fewer publishable papers. There is also the danger of losing subscriptions because of the higher price. This may be of less concern in the long run because libraries will not drop a serial solely because of a price increase unless it is underutilized; within limits, important scientific journals will continue to find space on library shelves. The short-term and long-term advantages of publishing extra issues are both signifi-

cant. Not only will authors have their material published more rapidly, the increased exposure of the journal to the scientific community may stimulate its growth even further. But although the initial impetus to publish more issues may be based on a temporary change in manuscript flow or acceptance rate, before taking this major step the editors and publisher must be prepared and willing to expand publication on a long-term basis.

6) Use careful editing to keep manuscripts down in length. Most scientific papers can be readily reduced by eliminating tables, or figures, or a lengthy decription. We shall return to this topic.

Editors may find themselves in a "Catch-22" situation in trying to maintain a balance between journal size and acceptance of papers. Being too rigid can turn authors away from a journal; being too easy may damage a journal's scientific credibility.

How does one monitor the size of the volume so that editorial brakes may be applied early enough to keep within a prescribed budget? If a decision has been made to limit each issue to x number of pages, the problem is relatively easy. Where the number of pages to be published in a given year is open-ended within limits, some care must be taken; the number of pages printed in the second half or last quarter of a calendar year, for example, will have to be reduced if early issues in a year are large. It is important to avoid, as much as possible, wide variations in the number of pages from one issue to another. Let us consider the case of a journal published bimonthly. By the time one has enough information to make a valid cost analysis of the first two issues, for example, January and March, commitments have already been made for the May issue and perhaps even for the July issue. On the basis of the number of pages already published and the costs per individual page, and knowing the average length of each article, it is possible to calculate the number of pages that one can publish during the rest of the year to keep within the stated budget. It is of interest that over an eight-year period for the *Journal of Lipid Research* the mean article size has been quite constant: 7.5–8.5 pages, equivalent to 5600–6600 words. For one of the journals referred to earlier the average article length over a six-year period was 8.8 pages. Of course, if one sees in July, for example, that reprint income is up and that subscription income is higher than in the budget, it may be possible to increase the number of pages to be printed and still remain within the total production budget for the journal.

SCIENTIFIC EDITING

Although all the functions of an editor may not have been satisfactorily defined, one general function is universally agreed upon. Woodford, in his article on training professional editors for scientific journals (1), stated "the function of an editor is to control quality in his journal." He mentions three areas of quality control; scientific worth, comprehensibility, and retrievability. Quality control of comprehensibility can directly affect the expenses of the journal. In a symposium in 1970 (2) on the rising costs of editing, Walters, then Director of the University of Alabama Press, wrote "increased specialization in academic training over the past 25 years has had a tendency to reduce literacy." Halpenny, another writer on the editorial process, has said "the sad truth is that the manuscripts of solid authors are rare in scholarly writing and appear much too seldom on the desks of editors" (3). Scientific writing is often done under the most unfavorable conditions. Scientists write against the demands of teaching, grant applications, seminars, committees, research, family routines, supervision, etc., and though it is reasonable to expect competent scientists to be able to write in a manner that will be understood by other scientists, this is not always the case. Some editors may be disinclined to accept a manuscript that requires extensive editorial attention. On the other hand, some journals are concerned with quality control over comprehensibility and will spend considerable time and money to edit scientifically acceptable manuscripts. One must ask how much editing is enough, since this editorial attention does contribute to costs. The best written paper will take only a short time to read and edit. Others may take several hours. A point of diminishing returns may be reached and further expenditure of time may not result in a commensurate benefit to the author and reader.

OTHER EDITORIAL PROCEDURES

In addition to the most significant expenses in editorial operations, other practices contribute somewhat less significantly to the overall costs. Reference checking is an important editorial function that is not overly expensive but may be overlooked or eliminated if a journal wishes to tighten up its operation. A qualified reference checker, whether a secretary, laboratory technician, or copy editor can verify 10 or 12 references an hour at a cost of $3.50–6.00 per hour. The average paper has 28 references, which can be checked in 2–2½ hours at a cost of about $7–$15 per paper.

The crisscrossing of reviews, that is, sending to one reviewer the comments of a second, is a valuable procedure that is not only quite educational for the reviewers but is also a courtesy. The reviewers have spent considerable time in evaluating a manuscript and should be provided with information about its disposition. The procedure is not difficult if the manuscript folder is set up from the beginning with this

TABLE 1.   Distribution of income by percentage

	Journal A	Journal B
Subscriptions	58–66*	62–77
Single issues		1–6
Reprints	10–14	19–29
Page charges	19–24	—
Manuscript fees	—	1
Interest	2	1–3
Miscellaneous	2	© 1

* Includes subscriptions and single issues.

TABLE 2.   Income and expense attributions

Income		Expense	
Authors (20–30%)	Subscribers (64–85%)	Authors (33–40%)	Subscribers (60–67%)
Reprints	Subscribers	Redactory	Circulation
Manuscript charges	Single issue sales	Reprint costs	Production
Miscellaneous	Interest	60% editorial office	40% editorial office

procedure in mind, but it can be somewhat time-consuming and therefore would contribute to the costs of the editorial assistant or secretary.

FINANCIAL ANALYSES

Since a journal serves both authors and subscribers, one may properly allocate income and expenses ascribable to authors and subscribers. Having done this, one may then derive internal financial variables that can be useful in analyzing journal operations from year to year. For example, various categories of income of a journal are shown in Table 1. These, and expenses, can be further classified, as shown in Table 2. It is clear that authors generate relatively more expense than income, while subscribers generate relatively more income than expense.

Table 3 illustrates other types of financial information that can be derived from the income and expense items, the number of subscribers, and the number of pages printed per year. These data are for three different years.

The difference between author income per page and author expense per page is the profit or loss per page ascribable to authors. Journals that have page charges are

TABLE 3.   Financial data on a journal for three years

	Dollars		
Total income/page	152.82	175.59	228.89
Total expenses/page	148.41	177.19	210.50
Profit (loss)/page	4.41	(1.60)	18.39
Author income/page	40.26	43.89	45.34
Author expenses/page	54.02	69.73	84.77
Profit (loss)/page	(13.76)	(25.84)	(39.43)
Profit (loss)	(9,962)	(16,434)	(19,163)
Subscriber income/subscriber	31.45	32.80	35.94
Subscriber expenses/subscriber	26.36	26.76	24.62
Profit (loss)/subscriber	5.09	6.04	11.32
Profit (loss)	13,188	15,426	28,096
Total profit (loss)	3226	(1008)	8933

likely to show a profit; those without page charges will usually show a loss. These profit or loss figures may be used as internal guides for adjusting reprint or page charges. However, it is unlikely that author-derived income can equal or exceed author-derived expense unless mandatory pages charges and/or manuscript handling fees are applied. This approach may be feasible for highly prestigious journals with a relatively large circulation that are assured of publishing several thousand pages a year. On the other hand, mandatory charges may be a questionable approach for smaller journals with lower circulation that publish under a thousand pages a year. This is especially true if a relatively large number of manuscripts from outside the United States are submitted and published. Effects of mandatory charges on foreign authors must be carefully considered. Author-derived income can also be increased by raising prices of reprints. This may be counterproductive, however, because as reprint costs rise, fewer are ordered by authors, although the percentage of authors ordering reprints may be constant. The effect may be a more or less steady net income. An economically feasible change may be to decrease substantially the price of reprints, especially if subscription prices are to be raised; this could increase net profits if more authors order an increased number of reprints. A decrease in reprint charges may also stimulate the rate of manuscript submissions.

Table 3 also depicts a similar analysis of subscriber income and expenses. The bottom-line figure in this analysis will usually show a net profit; it is the subscriber who really supports the journal.

These types of data are of interest and are useful in year-to-year comparisons. However, for a realistic appraisal of how a journal may fare in the marketplace of the scientific community, other editorial and financial considerations may be more significant. Table 4 compares two journals with respect to the number of issues, pages, and articles published each year, as well as what a subscription dollar buys. Journal A is owned by a large commercial publisher in Holland. Journal B is owned by a small nonprofit organization. Both journals are highly specialized in subject matter and publish the same types of articles. In a sense they are in direct competition. Assuming that the scientific merit of the papers in each journal is the same, it would appear that in 1976 and 1980 Journal B subscribers received more for their money than Journal A subscribers. Both journals doubled their subscription price in the four-year period, but Journal B published 44% more articles in 1980, whereas the increase for Journal A was 24%. With Journal A used as a point of reference, it appears that Journal B had considerable leeway for a price increase over and above the 1980 charge if only the unit cost (per article) to the subscriber is considered. On the other hand, Journal B reprints are expensive, whereas those for Journal A are not. Thus Journal A subscribers are, in a sense, subsidizing the cost of reprints for the authors. The 1982 figures in Table 4 are estimates based on the first six issues of each journal. In 1981 Journal A changed its format to a larger page size. Thus the 1982 parameters for this journal cannot be directly compared with those for 1976 and 1980. Moreover the subscription rate for Journal A in 1982 was 1.5% lower than in 1980. Although it is not possible to define the exact facts and figures that were used to determine the dollar price structure for 1982, certainly one consideration was the difference in the rate of currency exchange between 1980 and 1982. A

TABLE 4.   Comparison of two journals

Journal	1976		1980		1982[a]	
	A	B	A	B	A[b]	B
Articles published[c]	202	86	251	124	262	154
Total pages[d]	2106	658	2379	1014	2114	1276
Pages/article	10.4	7.6	9.5	8.2	8.1	8.3
Words/page[e]	560	860	560	860	750	860
Issues	12	6	12	8	12	9
Articles/issue	16.8	14.3	20.9	15.5	21.8	17.1
Pages/issue	176	110	198	127	176	142
Subscription price, $[f]	170	40	328	80	323	110
Price/issue, $	14.17	6.67	27.33	10.00	26.92	12.22
Price/article, $	0.84	0.47	1.31	0.65	1.23	0.71
Articles/$	1.19	2.15	0.77	1.82	0.81	1.40

[a] Estimates based on first 6 issues in 1982.
[b] Format changed to larger page size in 1981.
[c] Includes only original reports; journal also publishes 2–4 review articles per year.
[d] Based on pagination of included articles.
[e] Approximate; text only.
[f] Annual institutional cost.

Dutch guilder in July 1982 cost about 30% less, in terms of dollars, than in July 1980. Thus the relatively low price for Journal A in 1982 reflects the strong position of the U.S. dollar rather than a real price decrease. Even with the 37.5% increase (over a 2-year period) in the price for Journal B (with a 12.5% increase in the number of issues published annually and a projected 24% increase in the number of articles published), the Journal B institutional subscriber in 1982 can provide its readers with 1.4 articles for each dollar spent compared with 0.8 for Journal A, a difference of nearly 73%. The type of analysis shown in Table 4 can be readily accomplished for any journal and may provide valuable information. All one needs is a complete annual set of issues and the subscription prices.

An editor must record much other statistical information of a nonfinancial nature; review time, lead time for publication, average number of pages per article, submission rate, acceptance rate, geographical distribution of manuscripts, distribution of subject areas, good reviewers, poor reviewers, etc. These editorial exercises are a welcome change from the other chores natural in scientific editing. The information can be invaluable in setting editorial policies and establishing priorities that can affect financial stability and the quality of published papers.

THE COMPUTER IN THE EDITORIAL OFFICE

For many years both large and small editorial operations have utilized mainframe or minicomputers, often part of a large computer facility, for subscription fulfillment and fiscal management, as well as for text processing and manuscript management. Now as a result of the revolution in microcomputer technology, both hardware and software, and the increased awareness of what computers can do, more and more editorial offices will begin to acquire their own computer capabilities. Not only are microcomputers and peripheral hardware affordable by most journals, but the development of sophisticated yet "friendly" software has made it possible for even the computer novice to perform many types of operations, often with little or no assistance from professional programmers. The word processor may be one's first exposure to computer technology. It is difficult to envision a modern office without word-processing capability, whether it is in the form of a dedicated word processor or a true computer. The use of word processing in an editorial milieu has been discussed elsewhere (e.g., ref. 4 and 5) and is not treated further in this chapter.

Word processing, whether used for letters, manuscript revisions, or preparing reports, is but one use for the microcomputer. The full potential of the computer in editorial offices is realized only when it is used to process and manage the various types of information needed for a successful editorial operation. For years journals have relied on such devices as log books, card file systems, display boards, and ledgers for record keeping, manuscript management, and financial operations. Using computers for these purposes is not new. An editorial in *Biochemistry* in 1979 (6) described a rather sophisticated computer system for handling editorial files for that journal. The programs are written in Basic, and three users can simultaneously access data and run programs. Other, smaller journals have used microcomputers for similar purposes, with programs also written in Basic; however, the hardware allows only one user at a time. Microcomputer software that allows direct, effective, and efficient management and utilization of the data generated in journal operations is relatively new. For each manuscript that is submitted, sent out for review, and accepted for publication or rejected, numerous pieces of data are generated. These data customarily have been stored in various types of paper files. Some data may be regarded as archival; other data are needed for daily operation of the journal; perhaps some information is never used because there is no identified need for it; or some data that might be useful are too difficult to retrieve and/or collate because the appropriate file was not prepared. The value of all these data ultimately depends on the use to which they are put. Each person in an editorial operation has a different need and use for the data. A scientific editor or an associate editor may need to identify reviewers for a particular type of manuscript and to ascertain the general quality of the reviews of a given referee and how rapidly he or she returns the critique. An editorial assistant would need the addresses and phone numbers of reviewers. A managing or executive editor might need to know the average length of each published paper or average number of reprints ordered. How many papers concerned with a specific subject are being submitted to the journal? How many of such papers are accepted? Such information would be valuable if a journal wanted to attract papers of that particular subject. How many manuscripts contain electron micrographs, for example? What will be the economic impact if the quality of paper is upgraded to improve reproduction and perhaps attract additional manuscripts?

Computer data-base technology offers solutions for each end user (editor, managing editor, editorial assistant, etc.) to use the same data base to answer his or her particular question. A major advantage of data-base software is that its built-in programs can be used to generate specific programs for specific tasks and minimize or even eliminate the need for more complicated programs in Basic or other languages. One can envision any number of data bases, all linked together by one or more common denominators. One data base (or file) may contain information about each submitted manuscript, e.g., identification number; title; laboratory; authors (names, addresses, and phone numbers); key words; and number of figures, tables, halftones, electron micrographs, and references. A second data base may include the manuscript identification number, date of receipt, reviewer identification codes, dates when papers are sent out for review, dates when reviews are received, quality of the review, decision, date(s) of revision(s), and whether the manuscript is accepted or rejected. A third data base may contain the reviewer identification codes and the names, addresses, and phone numbers of reviewers, as well as their areas of expertise. Files could be set up for other types of information (e.g., contents of individual issues). With well-planned data bases and with well-formed ideas of the questions to be asked (perhaps the services of a programmer will be needed to get started), the end user will have a powerful tool. For example, it would be possible to identify reviewers for particular manuscripts and to generate mailing labels. It would be possible to keep track of all manuscripts and to update information on each manuscript or reviewer. In conjunction with word-processing programs, any number of reports, letters, labels, or forms can be generated. Furthermore there are programs available that will write specific types of programs based on what is typed onto the screen.

Nevertheless there are some drawbacks. There is the possible need for professional programming if packaged software is not available for a particular application or if the users are not trained in relatively simple programming. It would undoubtedly be necessary to enter a large data base before the full potential of the computer could be realized. This would mean transferring many of the paper files to the computer. The costs for programming and data entry will vary according to individual needs and experience and could be appreciable. Personnel time for programmers, analysts, or consultants may be $20–$75 per hour. The cost for data entry and verification may be on the order of $2 per 1000 keystrokes. Hardware costs may vary from about $5000 to $15,000 (including a printer) depending on sophistication. Maintenance should be budgeted at approximately 1% of the cost of the equipment per month. Software costs may be as high as $1500–$2000.

The microcomputer in conjunction with word processing and data-base management allows information to be retrieved and utilized in an innovative manner and offers the potential for very important and significant applications that can influence journal operations and economics.

REFERENCES

1. Woodford, F. P. Training professional editors for scientific journals. Sch. Publ. 2(1):41–46; 1970.
2. Walters, M. L. The rising cost of editing. Sch. Publ. 1(4):359–361; 1970.
3. Halpenny, F. G. Of time and the editor. Sch. Publ. 1(2):159–169; 1970.
4. Camps-Linney, T. Microcomputers in the editorial office. Earth and Life Science Editing. Sept. 1981, No. 14:4–6; 1981.
5. Smith, C. L. Word-processing management: A new role for the author's editor. CBE Views 5(1):8–11; 1982.
6. Neurath, H.; Garson, L. Editorial:Computer system for *Biochemistry*. Biochemistry 18: 5035–5037; 1979.

Copy Editing

MARGARET BROADBENT

Although style manuals and other specialized books describe in some detail the functions of copy editing and the attributes of good copy editors (1–5), only recently have articles appeared that deal with the economics of copy editing (6–13). What follows concerns the economics of copy editing chiefly from the point of view of conventional practices at a university press that publishes five monthly archival journals.

So far no machine has successfully scanned manuscripts for incorrect grammar, ambiguous phrasing, and inconsistencies in text and illustrative data. Copy editing, in the jargon of today, is labor intensive and consequently not a minor expense in the publishing process. For example, during 1980–81, copy editing represented 9.9% of the total publishing costs of the five journals produced by the Rockefeller University Press (Table 1). Faced with inflation, managing editors, publishers, and supporting societies are scrutinizing the economics of this salary-oriented operation and are asking, what are some of the considerations in controlling the cost of copy editing?

A basic and first consideration is to determine the quality desired in the printed journal. Does the editorial board wish a published paper to reflect an author's individual mode of expression? Or should all papers in a journal follow the more formal guidelines of Gowers' Fowler (14)? If sentences are to require recasting by the redactory service, and not by the editor, a specialized copy editor with a science background will be needed. Since the printer and the author both read galleys, how many more proofreadings by the copy editor are economically practical? What about the accuracy of bibliographic references? Seldom does the author submit them free from error. Should the redactory office verify references or should the author be held responsible for their accuracy? Answers to these questions directly affect quality and cost of copy editing.

Abstracts presented at annual meetings are commonly reproduced directly from authors' typescript. With proper guidelines, camera-ready tables and statistical data can also be provided by the author. Such copy not only eliminates copy editing but saves the expense of printer's composition. There is no definitive answer about quality; each editor or society will have to weigh the practical values of production time and savings to be gained against the degree of quality to be lost.

The author, editor, and printer can greatly affect the amount of copy editing required. *Scientific Writing for Graduate Students* (15) and style manuals such as those published by the Council of Biology Editors (16) and the American Psychological Association (17) were published to encourage the submission for publication of well-written papers presented in a standard form and style. The journal that regularly publishes specific instructions to authors requires less copy editing than the journal that does not furnish instructions. For example, manuscripts with reference citations typed with double spacing and in proper sequence, artwork drawn to proper scale, explanations of unusual abbreviations and acronyms, and trade names accompanied by the manufacturer's name and geographic location are a joy to copy editors.

High marks to the editor or his reviewer who notes on a typescript a new style convention officially adopted by a scientific society; highest marks, if a copy of the document, or a reference to it, accompanies the notation! The editor who recognizes ambiguous "zeros" or "ohs," "els," or "ones" saves copy editing time and possible alterations in proof. A few guidelines given to editors in advance about clarifying scientific data and SI units not only save copy editing time but assure that proof will be more accurate and authors happier. A regular flow of manuscripts from the editor to the redactory office provides economic use of copy editing time; a crash program for handling late manuscripts is expensive. A redactory office should always provide an editor with an annual schedule of deadlines for manuscripts.

Regular communication with the printer will quickly uncover overmarked copy, which not only increases the cost of copy editing but slows the printer's compositor and results indirectly in higher printing rates. Undermarked or poorly marked copy increases alteration charges. An occasional meeting of copy editors with the printer's technical staff can be very productive. Recently one of our printers conducted a workshop for copy editors on marking manuscripts for the computer. Our first reaction was that we had been "had" with a customer-do-it technique, but after styling several manuscripts, the copy editors agreed that the new system saved time! This system involves marking manuscripts with special codes, called formats, in which are embedded the formal type specifications. Another, more complicated form of marking is involved when the publisher provides the printer with a machine-readable tape. In this instance, the copy editor must insert specific codes to enable the computer to produce italics, superscripts, subscripts, etc., in the printed material.

Finally, within the redactory office itself, what is the best approach to the managing of copy editing? The volume of publication bears directly on this aspect since, for example, in an office producing only one journal, the number of copy editors may vary from less than one to several. For a redactory office with a staff to copy edit several journals, the production-line technique appears at first glance to be the most efficient. Under such conditions, assignments are by task or combination of tasks, with one individual assigned to overall schedules, or to styling references and mechanical typography, or to planning art work, or to proofreading, or to copy editing the text. Such a system by sheer repetitiveness assures individual proficiency as well as an opportunity for the individual to go from a simple to a more complex task. A person's special talents can also be fitted to an appropriate phase: organizational ability for scheduling, artistic ability for illustrations, detail orientation for proofreading. However, unless the publisher provides fairly rapid advancement, the worker becomes restive and the turnover in personnel is frequent. Staff backup for a task-oriented operation can present serious problems as well.

At the other end of the spectrum and in contrast to the "horizontal" task system is the vertical organization, where, under supervision, a copy editor is trained from the beginning to style manuscripts, size figures, and handle schedules for specific manuscripts. When proof of these papers arrives, the copy editor learns how to check galleys and pages. Within 14 months, such trainees, all college graduates, can become full production editors with complete responsibility for a single small journal, or a section of a larger one, following about a dozen papers from manuscript to final publication. The operation actually entails controlling each month about 36 papers distributed among three issues at various production stages. With this method, trainees learn fast; they acquire from the onset a perspective of the publishing operation. There is no time for copy editing overkill, Harman's "mystique of copy editing" (9). Well-chosen copy editors respond to responsibility; the turnover rate is low, with service averaging 2.5 to 3 years. Perhaps the greatest value of this system is the flexible interplay of copy editors who can assist others pressed with deadlines. Standard form and style and standard procedures throughout the office also make this possible. Occasional shifts to a position as senior production editor of a journal, to another journal, to special supplements, or to indexing jobs provide a copy editor with a change of pace and a broader grasp of scientific terms and publishing functions. However, the method does require an unassigned supervisor to train new copy editors and to oversee quality control; for the small publishing office it offers less opportunity for advancement than the task-oriented method.

Judicious use of freelance copy editors reduces institutional overhead, a fairly sizable item (Table 1). Our own Journals Office calls on one or two freelance people to copy edit manuscripts. However, with monthly journals and 48-hour turnaround time, there is no substitute for copy editors within an office to keep about 300 articles per month at various production stages moving.

TABLE 1. Distribution of expenses for five monthly journals published by The Rockefeller University Press

Expenditure	%
Editorial	12.1
Copy editing	9.9
Printing	53.7
Distribution and subscription service	13.8
Administrative, clerical	3.9
Rockefeller University overhead*	6.6
	100

*Includes general services. Fringe benefits are included in specific items.

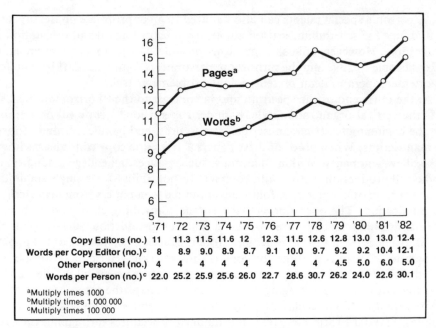

	'71	'72	'73	'74	'75	'76	'77	'78	'79	'80	'81	'82
Copy Editors (no.)	11	11.3	11.5	11.6	12	12.3	11.5	12.6	12.8	13.0	13.0	12.4
Words per Copy Editor (no.)[c]	8	8.9	9.0	8.9	8.7	9.1	10.0	9.7	9.2	9.2	10.4	12.1
Other Personnel (no.)	4	4	4	4	4	4	4	4	4.5	5.0	6.0	5.0
Words per Person (no.)[c]	22.0	25.2	25.9	25.6	26.0	22.7	28.6	30.7	26.2	24.0	22.6	30.1

[a]Multiply times 1000
[b]Multiply times 1 000 000
[c]Multiply times 100 000

Fig. 1.   Productivity of journal copy editors over a 12-year period.

Figure 1 shows improved productivity of Rockefeller journal copy editors over a 12-year period, chiefly by simplifying mechanical marking for the printer; receiving better copy from the authors, such as camera-ready tables and symposium abstracts; employing freelance copy editors; and reducing the turnover rate of personnel.

How are copy editing costs computed for any one journal? The simplest but most costly way would be to assign copy editors rigidly to specific journals. However, with a pool of copy editors, the total copy editing costs of a redactory office can be apportioned on the basis of annual volume of characters, or words, published per journal. We find this method quite satisfactory owing to standard style and procedures used in the office. The count of characters or words per page is occasionally adjusted, by actual time and motion studies, for the journal that makes special time demands, such as one containing a large proportion of critical halftone illustrations.

With the new technology, the copy editor is assuming more responsibility in shepherding the manuscript through the computer process, which reduces composition cost at the printing plant. For example, the redactory service is working with the Rockefeller computer facilities to supply computer-readable tapes for special journal sections and indexes. The tapes can be immediately converted into camera-ready pages for the printing press. Corrections are easily merged in the new memory technology, thus simplifying the work of the copy editor in handling proof.

It is evident that the author, editor, and copy editor are each becoming more accustomed to the word processor and computer that enable the swift and accurate manipulation of the material, with promise of economies in the publishing process. The publisher or society will continue to weigh the value of quality copy editing versus the practicalities of production time and expense. The publishing and editing offices that communicate pertinent and lucid instructions to authors will be encouraging quality writing by the author and the submission of typescript of acceptable standard form and style.

The traditional role of the copy editor is bound to be modified. With the advent of on-demand wire information like that proposed by Comtext, it is too early to forecast at what stage, if any, the on-line computerized text would require copy editing for video screen reading and for the microfiche and printed spinoffs. The trend clearly will put more responsibility for quality presentation on the author.

Bradley Hundley and Raymond Fastiggi of The Rockefeller University Press generously provided information and updated statistics on the current copy editing operation.

REFERENCES

1. A manual of style. 12th ed. Chicago, IL: Univ. of Chicago Press; 1969; pp. 40–55.
2. Skillin, M.E. Words into type. 3rd ed. Englewood Cliffs, NJ: Prentice-Hall, Inc.; 1974; pp. 59–61.
3. Butcher, J. Copy-editing: the Cambridge handbook. London: Cambridge Univ. Press; pp. 1–3.
4. DeBakey, L. The scientific journal. Editorial policies and practices. St. Louis, MO: C. V. Mosby Company; 1976; pp. 91–93.
5. Day, R. A. How to write and publish a scientific paper. Philadelphia, PA: ISI Press; 1979.
6. Core, G. Costs and copy-editing. Sch. Publ. 6:59–65; 1974.
7. Bauer, G.; Harvey, W. B.; James, R.; Jones, T. L.; Kefauver, W. A.; Morin, A. J.; Welch, S.; Raab, C.; Unwin, R.; Walters, M. L. Sch. Publ. 1:347–361; 1970.
8. Stith, M. E.; Pascal, N. B.; Wiley, L. M.; Kubec, J. E. The out-of-house editor, a four-part article. Sch. Publ. 3:259–272; 1972.
9. Harman, E. T. A reconsideration of manuscript editing. Sch. Publ. 7:146–156; 1976.
10. DeVivo, A. Copyediting standards at the American Psychological Association. IEEE Trans. Prof. Commun. PC–18:141–144; 1975.
11. National Academy of Sciences, Committee on Scientific and Technical Communication. Report of the task group on the economics of primary publication. Washington, DC: National Academy of Sciences; 1970.
12. Council of Biology Editors, Committee on Economics. Economics of scientific publications. Bethesda, MD: Council of Biology Editors, Inc.; 1973.
13. Aspen Systems Corporation. Interim report on the project "Editorial processing centers —operational experiments." Germantown, MD: Aspen Systems Corporation; No. 5262, 1976.
14. Fowler, H. W. A dictionary of modern English usage. 2nd ed. Revised by E. Gowers. New York: Oxford Univ. Press; 1965.

15. Council of Biology Editors, Committee on Graduate Training in Scientific Writing. Scientific writing for graduate students. Bethesda, MD: Council of Biology Editors, Inc.; 1976.
16. Council of Biology Editors, Committee on Form and Style. CBE style manual. 4th ed. Bethesda, MD: Council of Biology Editors, Inc.; 1978.
17. Publication manual of the American Psychological Association. 2nd ed. Washington, DC: American Psychological Association; 1972.

Purchasing Typesetting Separately from Printing

JOANNE FETZNER

With the ever-increasing capability, flexibility, and availability of phototypesetting systems, more and more printers of scientific journals are acquiring the necessary equipment to convert journals that have historically been limited to Monotype hot-metal composition to the newer, more cost-efficient methods provided by computer-aided photocomposition. But because most of these printers have had a sizable investment in existing hot-metal equipment, the conversion has not been as rapid as it might have been if the old technology were not already adequate to do the job. However, because phototypesetting makes it possible to separate the typesetting and printing production processes, two parallel trends have emerged to speed the conversion. 1) Large-volume publishers have purchased in-house systems and are enjoying the benefits of increased control, improved scheduling, and reduced cost. 2) Commercial typesetting companies without capital invested in either antiquated hot-metal machines or printing and binding plants have made these benefits of computer-aided phototypesetting available to small-volume publishers who can separate their composition and printing production processes.

A SPLIT PRODUCTION SYSTEM

Typesetting and printing can be functionally separated according to a journal's needs in each area. Without the physical requirements that previously linked the two processes (hot metal), acquiring the first copy of a journal (i.e., composition) can be accomplished quite independently of the acquisition and distribution of the next 5000 or 50,000, since camera-ready copy or negatives can be easily and inexpensively shipped to the printer who fulfills the special printing needs of a particular publication.

The physical characteristics of a journal are probably the most obvious reason for choosing separate suppliers for typesetting and printing. For example, a technical journal may require very sophisticated composition that is available from a limited number of typesetters, but for printing, require a small sheet-fed press, a small press run, and minimum storage for back issues—requirements that can be met by a multitude of printers from whom the most economical bid can be chosen. The second, not-so-obvious reason for choosing separate suppliers is location, because the

should be located near the publisher and the printer near
nsity of subscribers for distribution-related economies.
es (equipment and capability, and location) will often ne-
arate suppliers, particularly if the other variables usually
aluation of journal production bids—namely, overall qual-
cially price—are also improved by this choice. For example,
it w... o settle for composition that is not the most sophisticated in
return for an ccc al printing package, or conversely, to pay more for printing
in order to achieve the desired quality in composition. The luxury of a single supplier
is no longer cost-effective because large printers with typesetting capabilities are
streamlining their manufacturing plants and will be offering fewer printing options
to publishers. Thus a publisher might pay more for the required typesetting capability when restricting the choice of supplier to those printers offering the options
needed for an economical printing price. With the ever-widening range in available
typesetting sophistication, the most suitable typesetting for a particular journal or
group of journals, at the best price, and the most suitable printing, at the best price,
will almost never be achieved in a single contract. Contracting with separate suppliers allows the publisher to change only one production process at a time, thus limit-
ing the unforeseen problems created when any production change is made. Bids
should be solicited frequently for both typesetting and printing, but not in the same
year for both.

BUYING TYPESETTING

There are basically three ways to buy typesetting: 1) purchase a complete in-
house system; 2) buy the complete typesetting process, from marked and edited copy
through camera-ready pages or negatives, from a commercial compositor; or 3)
bring a cost-effective portion of the typesetting process in-house and use a commercial typesetter for the remaining tasks.

The decision as to whether to purchase a complete in-house system should be
based on the volume of typesetting required and the staffing available to run the system. For the small-volume publisher (under 5000 pages per year), a small integrated
system (formerly called a direct-input phototypesetter, until floppy-disk storage was
added to allow copy to be input, saved, and typeset later) would be adequate. This
could involve an investment of as little as $50,000, but these small systems are very
unsophisticated, very labor-intensive, and often incapable of setting scientific material. It is possible, of course, to produce acceptable camera copy with these systems
(indeed the earliest journals to abandon hot-metal typesetting for phototypesetting
were produced on these systems), but they are very slow and very dumb, requiring
the user to be knowledgeable about typesetting and willing to spend a great deal of
time setting copy. But for straight, uncomplicated copy, their return-on-investment
time, excluding personnel costs, is very short (1–2 years).

For the large-volume publisher (10,000 pages and up per year), the picture is
considerably brighter for purchasing a complete in-house system. The choice is
clearly a large integrated sytem, including a smart front-end system and a digital

typesetter. These require an investment of between $130,000 and $200,000, depending on whether a backup system is included and on the level of sophistication of both the front-end system and the typesetter. They are infinitely more automated, including in some cases the capability of page makeup before typesetting, but precisely because of this vastly increased capability and flexibility, even more typesetting knowledge is required to use the system to its full capacity. If the volume is there, however, and experience and expertise with the system are achieved, these large systems can be very cost-effective over a period of a few years.

While the reduced typesetting cost is a primary concern to publishers considering the purchase of an in-house system, there are other significant advantages, including: 1) greater editorial control, 2) improved scheduling, 3) improved quality and an opportunity to effect design improvements once expertise has been attained on the system, and 4) the capability to more easily produce type for various corollary programs—advertising, direct mail, in-house promotion, brochures, meeting programs, etc. These benefits can be enjoyed by larger publishers who have the publication volume to support a large system and the capital necessary to purchase such a system. Most or all of these benefits, however, can also be enjoyed by a small publisher by contracting with a commercial typesetter. This arrangement can be preferable to a small in-house system because of the increased capability: 1) adjustments to the peaks and valleys of a journal's work flow are easier because a larger volume of work and faster service are possible; 2) the commercial typesetter probably has a backup system to pick up the slack of downtime on the main system; 3) more type variety is likely to be available, and certainly more sophisticated and automatic typography would be possible than with a small integrated in-house system. With this increased capability of the large integrated systems, the publisher can work with the typesetter to achieve greater editorial control and improved quality, which in some cases can reduce printing costs. Since the publisher is not buying a typesetting-printing package, it is easier to purchase type for a variety of other publishing activities, such as advertising and direct mail, for which the publisher will probably contract with a different printer from the one who prints the journals. Thus a small-volume publisher can achieve some of the cost reduction acclaimed by users of large in-house systems by separately and carefully choosing a commercial typesetter and can achieve some of the other benefits of in-house typesetting as well.

A compositor should be chosen whose equipment matches the physical requirements of the publication(s), including the degree of sophistication that will most automate the typesetting process, and whose quality, scheduling, and price are satisfactory. Since the technology of computer-aided photocomposition is changing and improving so rapidly, and in some cases actually reducing in cost, multiple bids should be evaluated frequently (once a year is not too often). A publisher may find himself changing typesetters for better quality and less cost simultaneously. For example, cost savings in author or editor alterations can result from greater front-end sophistication. A very smart front-end system (which includes computer intervention at the input stage) not only produces better typography the first time copy is set, but it can also make alterations easily and inexpensively, a savings that the typesetter can pass along to the publisher. Most of the larger systems currently available include a pretypesetting proofing capability, so the typesetter can correct errors before the material is typeset, making the galleys cleaner and proofreading and layout easier. Although technically publishers do not pay for printer's errors, the typesetter incurs costs in correcting keyboarding errors and typography errors (loose lines, incorrect hyphenation, widows, etc.) caused by a relatively ignorant front-end system, and these costs are built into the overall charges to the publisher. Consequently a smarter front-end system may result in lower typesetting charges to the publisher in the same way that alterations can be cheaper on an automated system.

For the small publisher who does not type manuscript copy, there are enough commercial typesetters with large systems appropriate for scientific journals with whom a contract could be arranged to provide many of the benefits of in-house composition.

The third alternative method of buying typesetting is especially suited to the small publisher who requires the sophistication of a large system but does not have the volume to support it. Bringing a cost-effective portion of the process in-house can save some costs incurred by contracting with a commercial typesetter for the entire composition process. This is accomplished by interfaced typesetting, using a word processor to communicate copy (either by telecommunication or physical disk delivery) to a smart front-end system and typesetter, thus moving the labor-intensive portion of the process into the publisher's office, where it can be less expensive, if the staffing is already available, than purchasing this process from the typesetter. The input can actually be easier on a word processor than on an in-house typesetter, because word processors have sophisticated editing features, and the larger front-end system, interfaced with the word processor, can supply simplified formats to input instead of complicated typographic codes.

For the small publisher, this hybrid system can provide the best of both worlds —certainly the increased control and probably some improved scheduling and reduced cost of an in-house preparation, and the sophisticated typesetting of a highly efficient front-end system. The best approach is to work backward from the composition system judged most appropriate for a specific journal's requirements, i.e., find a typesetter with an appropriate system who also has the capability of receiving electronic input (*not* a labor-intensive task). For example, a publisher may find a compositor using a highly sophisticated front-end system with a translation table to convert input from a specific microcomputer into a form readable by the system, so the hardware investment need not exceed the purchase of the micro (with word-processing software) and a modem for communication. A printer may be added for in-house proofreading before telecommunication or the typesetter may send back to the publisher's microcomputer a hyphenated, justified version of the input (in some cases, made up into pages) for proofing and editing prior to actual composition. With this system, type is set only once, thus saving time on the digital typesetter (and associated consumables) and time and labor on page makeup. Thus the commercial typesetter incurs neither of the two most labor-intensive portions of the typesetting process, i.e., keyboarding and layout and paste-up, and the publisher incurs only the keyboarding portion, which may be done by existing staff familiar with the journals being published. Even the initial keyboarding can eventually be done by the authors, as more and more people acquire word processors—the publisher can accept word-processor tapes, edit the manuscripts, add codes on the video-display terminal, and transmit by telecommunication to the commercial typesetter. The investment in such a hybrid system can be under $6000 for a microcomputer and software, printer, adequate memory, and modem for telecommunication. Although this system does move more preparation into the publisher's office, adding personnel cost to the hardware cost, it also provides the additional benefits of other uses for the microcomputer, particularly in circulation and financial management.

TYPESETTING CHANGES TO REDUCE OTHER PRODUCTION COSTS

Photocomposition allows multiple format changes that can reduce the other significant cost of journal manufacturing, i.e., printing. Although publishers routinely control costs by selecting the most economical printing contract every 2 or 3 years, little or no control can be obtained over some other production costs (paper and distribution), because a limit is soon reached on weight and quality of paper and because paper, postage, and other distribution costs continue to rise at an alarming rate. Since paper and distribution costs vary in direct proportion to the number of pages published, the single largest production savings comes from reducing the number of pages.

Some format changes that maximize the use of each printed page can actually improve the design and make a journal easier to read. Increased variety of type and style is less expensive with photocomposition than with hot-metal composition. Some digital typesetters have 500–1000 typefaces (in a range from 5 points to 75–100 points, in increments of $\frac{1}{10}$ or $\frac{1}{2}$ points, and in line lengths up to 100 picas) all immediately available and mixable on a given page of text. With this almost infinite variety, both readability and characters per page can be maximized before a single character is set. For example, most publishers still begin a new article on a new page rather than start a new article on the same page that ends another paper. With computer-assisted page makeup, which provides an electronic image of the page before typesetting, short pages could be virtually eliminated by simply rerunning the article with less leading to make the manuscript one page shorter. With the smart front-end systems on the market today, the use of small format deviations to achieve savings in printing costs is limited only by editorial judgment.

COORDINATION OF PRODUCTION SCHEDULES

When the typesetter is independent of the printer, the publisher must be responsible for coordinating the two manufacturing schedules to meet the final publication deadline for a particular journal issue. Production schedules should be drawn up in the usual fashion, working backward from the date a particular issue should arrive at the post office. The printer will determine the printing schedule and advise the publisher when he will need the camera copy, ads, halftones, etc. Then a schedule can be worked out between the publisher and the compositor, working backward from the date on which the printer needs the camera-ready text pages. Scheduling is no greater problem when working with multiple suppliers than it is when working with a single supplier — if the publisher makes a schedule and sticks to it and chooses suppliers who do likewise.

To put an entire issue together, using materials from various sources (halftones from the editor, ads from the advertisers, text from the typesetter), the printer needs press-planning instructions from the publisher. These instructions should include: 1) a list of all numbered and unnumbered text pages coming from the typesetter and when, 2) standing pages already at the printer, 3) titles and locations of halftones, 4) titles and locations of ads, 5) instructions for the covers, and 6) the press run. To ensure smooth sailing for each issue through the plant and to the post office, the printer should make these instructions available to all plant personnel working on the journal.

Each individual journal will have its own particular characteristics that will determine the feasibility of a split production process. A large number of halftones, especially if authors' proofs (sent from the compositor) must include halftone reproductions, may reduce the cost savings and increase the coordination problems if the halftones must be supplied by the printer. However, phototypesetting systems are getting smarter all the time, and some are already capable of producing graphics and halftones. These systems are quite expensive and only one currently has halftone capability in wide use. However, considering the dramatic improvements in computer-aided phototypesetting during the 1970's, it is quite easy to visualize a more widespread use of additional capabilities like halftones during the 1980's.

CONCLUSION

This chapter could not have been written 10 years ago; 10 years from now another will be needed to replace it. Although such a chapter may include a discussion of the computer-aided distribution of scientific information, in addition to computer-aided typesetting, the editorial and financial benefits of this new technology to traditional scientific journal publication will be even more substantial than it is in 1982. Since the universal availability and the permanent recording of scientific research are essential to the growth of scientific knowledge, the traditional scientific journal will continue to exist, perhaps alongside other media of scientific communication. However, the entire preprint evolution of research reports (including data analysis and interpretation, writing, editorial review and revision, typesetting, and even parallel electronic distribution) will probably be accomplished via microcomputers and telecommunication. The publishers who recognize this trend and the substantial benefits of this advanced technology even now in 1982 will be the ones making the greatest contribution to the dissemination of scientific knowledge in 1992.

Presswork, Binding, and Paper

ROBERT V. ORMES

Presswork, binding, and paper constitute three of the six major cost factors associated with journal manufacturing and distribution. The other three are *1*) composition, including typesetting, page makeup, prepress photography and other preparations for plate-making, and corrections; *2*) mailing, including wrapping, labeling, sorting, bundling, and sacking in accord with post office requirements; and *3*) postage.

For effective management of manufacturing, distribution, and evaluation of bids from prospective suppliers, it seems prudent to analyze each factor separately as well as together in light of the journal's particular mechanical requirements. Such analyses should enable a journal publisher, editor, or business manager to select the printer whose skills and equipment provide the best available match for the journal's requirements at the time the judgment must be made. They should also enable that person to make sound judgments about the effect on the match of changes in the journal's requirements or changes in the printer's equipment and hence to decide whether and when new arrangements for manufacturing should be considered.

A journal's mechanical requirements define its manufacturing needs. The main ones, once the design and page measurements have been established, are the number of pages, the number of issues, and the number of copies per issue. These numbers, when multiplied by the unit price for each applicable cost factor, provide a dollar amount for the year that shows the relative effect of each cost factor on the total costs and therefore which factors require the most time and attention for analysis. By way of illustration, consider two hypothetical journals of the same page and type size, both publishing 1152 pages per year in black ink, and both having separate covers and using the same grade and style of paper. One is published quarterly (288 pages per issue) in a run of 2000 copies. The other is published monthly (96 pages) in a run of 10,000 copies. Both are run on the same press, which has a page capacity of 32 pages and delivers one folded signature; both use the same paper; both require four press plates for each inside run. Obviously composition and other preparatory costs will· be about equal by year, though not by issue. Press plates will also cost nearly the same. However, press running time, paper consumption, and binding and mailing time will be considerably greater for the monthly.

With these data and some rough unit costs, we can construct a table for the two journals. All costs have risen substantially since this table was originally prepared, but the qualitative comparisons are still useful (Table 1).

For both journals, composition is by far the most important cost factor. Nevertheless, over the entire year the additional copies required by the monthly journal change the picture and show that paper and press running costs are larger cost factors in the monthly journal than they are in the quarterly journal. If the monthly had a circulation of 50,000, paper would become the largest cost factor (39%). Composition would drop to 34%, press plates to 8%. Press running costs would go up to 11% and binding and mailing to 3½%. For any journal, the first question about manufacturing costs is "What does the journal need?" and the second is "Who can meet these needs most economically?"

Printing presses are available in many different sizes with many different characteristics and combinations of characteristics and hence costs. Some will print 4 pages at a time, others 6, 8, 16, 32, 64, 96, or even 128. Some accept paper in sheets, some in rolls. Some have no attached folder. Some deliver a single folded signature. Others will deliver two, four, or eight folded signatures. Some can print a second color on any or all pages, and some can print a second color only by reducing the total page capacity by half. Some can print 2000 copies an hour, and others can print 20,000, 30,000 or more.

The larger, faster, and more complex the press configuration, the higher the hourly cost for labor, capital investment, and overhead, which is usually translated by printers' estimators into cost per 1000 copies. To these costs are usually added the cost of the ink required and sometimes the cost of the paper, which includes not only the actual cost of the paper but also a charge for spoilage or waste, a charge for handling and storage, a charge for the printer's investment, and a markup. Hence, in analyzing press running costs, one must ask a number of questions to determine what is included and what is not and what the relative weights of the different subfactors are.

The object of such study is to find a press that is complex enough to meet the journal's needs but not unnecessarily complex. Thus, if the journal does not run a second color at all, it should usually run on a one-color press. If it runs a small number of pages in two colors, analysis will show whether it is more economical to run all forms on a two-color press or all on a one-color press, with the two-color forms running at half the normal page capacity of the press, or most forms on a one-color press and the color forms on a different, two-color press. What you do depends on the printer's equipment, but some printers are almost certainly better equipped than others for handling any particular journal.

If the journal publishes editorial or advertising inserts, it may need a press with a fancy folder that delivers several signatures from each form and hence provides flexibility in placement of the inserts, but note that the additional signatures will increase costs in the bindery.

Other factors to be considered in analyzing the cost of presswork are the quality of the printing plates to be used for the job, the degree of automation of platemaking, the amount of ink needed, the efficiency of press utilization, and paper waste.

Printing plates should be of good enough quality to maintain the excellence of

TABLE 1. Cost comparisons for two hypothetical journals

	Quarterly			Monthly		
	Units	Cost ($)	%	Units	Cost ($)	%
Composition, etc. ($50 per page)						
By year	1,152 pp.	57,600	75	1,152 pp.	57,600	60
By issue	288 pp.	14,400		96 pp.	4,800	
Press plates, inside (8 pp. each) ($100 each)						
By year	144 pl.	14,400	19	144 pl.	14,400	15
By issue	36 pl.	3,600		12 pl.	1,200	
Press plates, cover ($50 each)						
By year	4 pl.	200	<1	12 pl.	600	<1
By issue	1 pl.	50		1 pl.	50	
Press running, inside ($10 per 1000 for each 32-page form)						
Copies	2,000			10,000		
By year	2 × 36 × $10	720	1	10 × 36 × $10	3,600	4
By issue	2 × 9 × $10	180		10 × 3 × $10	300	
Press running, cover ($8 per 1000)						
By year	4 (2 × $8)	64	<1	12 (10 × $8)	960	1
By issue	2 × $8	16		10 × $8	80	
Paper, inside (100 lb. for the first 1000 16's, 80 lb. for additional 1000's @ $24/cwt.)						
By year	12,960 lb	3,100	4	59,000 lb.	14,200	15
By issue	3,240 lb.	775		4,920 lb.	1,180	
Paper, cover ($10 per 1000)						
By year	4 (2 × 10)	80	<1	12 (10 × 10)	1,200	1
By issue	2 × 10	20		10 × 10	100	
Bindery setup ($80 each)						
By year	4	320	<1	12	960	1
By issue	1	80		1	80	
Bindery running ($10 per 1000 first three signatures and cover, $1 per 1000, each additional signature)						
By year	36 signatures	128	<1	36 signatures	1,200	1
By issue	9 signatures	32		3 signatures	100	
Mailing (not wrapped) ($10 per 1000)						
By year	8,000	80	<1	120,000	1,200	1
By issue	2,000	20		10,000	100	
Totals						
By year		76,692	100		95,920	100
By issue		19,173			7,990	

the ink impressions throughout the run but not longer. (Very long runs may require a set of replacement plates at the midpoint of the run.) Ask the printer the cost and run length of the plates he proposes to use for your job. If it seems relevant, also ask how he makes plates and how long it takes to make them. All the data and information you acquire will improve your knowledge and your ability to make appropriate analyses of needs and equipment in the future. Keep copies of the information obtained and your analyses; they may provide useful comparisons with future analyses.

Although the cost of ink is relatively small in short runs, it may be useful to know how many pounds are required for your journal's run. The printer can tell you. Many inks are petroleum-based, and therefore their prices are likely to increase more rapidly than some other prices. In addition, it is useful to ask about the drying qualities of the inks and the method used to dry them. Inks may be dried by passing the paper through a gas flame before it is folded, by passing it through an oven that may be heated by any one of several means, by passing paper inked with light-set inks under ultraviolet light, and by other means, including simple absorption by the paper. You may need to know these things if work on your journal is not to be delayed by fuel shortages or if you must adjust your specifications temporarily to meet a fuel shortage.

A press capacity should be sought that enables the journal to be printed at an average run as close to 100% of press capacity as possible. Thus if the best press for your journal seems to be one of 32-page capacity, make plans to maximize the number of 32-page runs and minimize runs of 8, 16, and 24 pages. Each of these runs takes as much press time as a 32-page run, and the hour cost is the same. There will probably be a small discount from the cost per 1000 for the fully efficient run, but the cost per page will nevertheless be signficantly higher (nearly double for a 16-page run). Do not forget, however, that plate costs will be lower for a 16-page run (two plates) than for a 32-page run (four plates). Even if you determine that a 32-page press is the best one for your job at a particular printing plant, do not conclude that this will be true at all printing plants. For example, if your average issue is 96 pages, three runs will be required on a 32-page press. But another printer may have a 48-page press, which requires only two runs. Such presses usually have three roll-stands for feeding the paper, and paper waste factors are higher and must be taken into consideration if a reasonable decision is to be made in favor of one or the other. Count your press runs, as well as your pages and copies.

Paper waste is much higher on the larger and more complex presses than it is on the smaller, less complex ones. The waste, or spoilage, factor is greater for two-color and four-color forms than it is for one-color forms. These costs are reflected in the prices charged for color pages. Waste factors also increase when half-sized rolls of paper must be used as, for example, in 8- and 24-page runs. Waste factors may be important in determining whether a sheet-fed press is the best equipment for your journal. Sheet-fed presses are slower, but paper waste is lower and paper prices per pound are higher (about 25% for the same grade). Ask your suppliers about waste factors, which are usually stated in percentage – that is, percentage of paper used.

The main determinants of cost in the bindery are the size of the binder that must be used and the time required to do the job. The binder is a long machine containing stations from which the signatures are fed in sequence until the complete copy is ready for pasting or stapling. If a large number of signatures is required, a long binder is required, as well as extra people to keep the different stations filled up with the proper signatures.

Many variables affect the cost of presswork, binding, and paper. Each one that has a significant effect on the total cost of a journal's production should be identified and analyzed if the journal is to be produced not only at a cost the journal can afford but also at a price that will attract the largest possible number of subscribers.

Distribution and Postage

George B. Roscoe

At present the most efficient and economical method of distributing scientific journals is through the Postal Service, but there is no guarantee that this will continue to be the case.

For almost two centuries these periodicals have enjoyed postal rates at levels far below cost. The public paid the difference through taxes. The situation started to change dramatically when the Congress enacted the Postal Service Reorganization Act of 1970, which decreed that *all* classes of mail must pay their own way. At that time only first class was doing so. To lessen the impact of sudden, huge postal cost increases to mailers who had benefited most from the subsidy, Congress laid out a program for gradual increases in periodic increments. Second-class regular rate mailers were given eight years to get used to the cost adjustments. Congress was particularly considerate of nonprofit special rate publishers, who include many scientific, education, and philanthropic periodicals. They were given 16 years, postponing the day of full reckoning until July 1987.

That day of reckoning may be much closer. In January 1982 the economy deteriorated and the nonprofit special rate was adjusted to the step 13 level; in the summer of 1982 all subsidies were stricken from the pending legislation for a time, but at the last minute they were reinstated at step 13 for a couple of months—until October 1, 1982. The resolution of the postal subsidy issue is very much in doubt, but the prevailing judgment indicates that any prudent planning must take into account an early end to subsidies and a steadily increasing cost for Postal Service magazine delivery. This will be an increasingly larger budget item in the years ahead.

DISTRIBUTION COST SAVINGS

Publishers should explore ways and means to save on distribution costs. Some organizations may find that truck or even airlifts directly from the printer to larger cities for dispatch from post offices may be possible. Some large commercial publishers already do this to a limited extent: shipping by truck to large cities and mailing to readers to take advantage of in-county and close-in zone rates. Airlifts to foreign countries where there is considerable circulation is another way to moderate high foreign postage costs and speed delivery. Contact the commercial departments of the airlines, particularly foreign carriers, and explain your problem. Further advantages may be possible by two or more smaller publishers consolidating their shipments to meet minimum weight requirements or gain volume discounts.

Some publishers have not availed themselves of substantial savings resulting from more careful mail preparation and the discount rates offered for presorting and doing other parts of the postal work. (See the rate section for second-class mail in the Domestic Mail Manual Section 411.212.)

USING THE U.S. POSTAL SERVICE

The U.S. Postal Service was created by the Postal Act of 1798 to facilitate dissemination of scientific, educational, informational, and agricultural knowledge throughout the land, with any deficits incurred to be met out of the U.S. Treasury. Because the days of billion dollar annual postal deficits are over and publishers will be picking up a substantial portion of this public saving, it behooves them to invest some time and effort in getting to know the postal system. Its bite from publishing budgets is moving in the direction of 20% of basic costs.

Here are two important first steps:

1) Visit your local postmaster and regional mail center where your publication is mailed. Discuss your publications, any problems, things you do not understand and ask his advice and assistance. Get to know the key people there, particularly those in charge of mail classification and transportation of second-class mail. Ask them to place your name on their mailing list so you will be alerted to changes in policy and procedure.

2) Subscribe to the Domestic Mail Manual (DMM), a looseleaf service that provides the only authoritative information on postal regulations. This is obtained by annual subscription of approximately $50 and may be ordered through the Superintendent of Documents, Government Printing Office, Washington, DC 20202. It includes about 700 pages in nine chapters but only two chapters (about 70 pages) are of main concern to the publisher—Chapter 4 (Second Class) and Chapter Six (Third Class). Updated supplements are sent out periodically to be substituted for out-of-date material and inserted in the binder much on the order of the Commerce Clearing House Services. The DMM is indexed and is quite readable and understandable.

There are four classifications of mail and a fifth service—E-Com (electronic computer-originated mail)—that publishers may use to advantage. The most important postal department to a publisher is the Mail Classifications Division at the U.S. Postal Service Headquarters, 475 L'Enfant Planza West, S.W., Washington, DC 20260. This unit administers regulations covering all types of mail. It is empowered to investigate admissibility, accepts or rejects mail, and holds hearings on appeals involving suspensions or rejections. It determines the type of material deemed to be of sufficient public interest to merit more favorable rates. Other major problems such as rates are fixed by the Postal Service and the Postal Rate Commission. The Mail Classification Division, Rates and Classifications Department, U. S. Postal Service, Washington, DC 20260 (phone 202-245-4542) and local postmasters are primary contact points.

Here are the mail classifications:

• First Class: Postal cards, post cards, sealed or unsealed letters containing written or typewritten matter, matter closed against postal inspection, and bills and statements of account.

• Second Class: Newspaper and other periodical publications such as magazines. (See DMM 421.1 for detailed definition of periodicals.) Second-class postage fees are paid for in two ways: *1*) a charge per piece and *2*) another charge per pound (advertising content is divided into postal zones and charged for accordingly). A lesser per pound charge is assessed for editorial content. There are two general rate structures: *1*) regular (commercial), and *2*) nonprofit special rate.

• Third Class: Mailable matter that is not required to be mailed at first class, is not entered as second-class mail, and weighs less than 16 ounces. This mail includes circulars, identical letters to several persons, printed matter within the third-class weight limit, and merchandise samples.

• Fourth Class: Merchandise, printed matter, mailable live animals, and all other matter not included in first, second, or third class.

• E-Com Service: Electronic computer-originated mail is a subclass of first class. It consists of mail entered into the postal system at designated serving post offices by electronic means via communications common carriers.

Some Key Provisions in the Domestic Mail Manual

Newspapers and other periodicals that meet criteria established in DMM Section 123 may be mailed at second-class rates if they are issued regularly at least four times a year. They must be issued and mailed from a known office of publication; must be formed of printed sheets; must have contents originated and published to disseminate information of a public character or be devoted to literature, the sciences, art, or some industry and have a legitimate list of paid subscribers; must not be designed primarily for advertising (more than 75% in more than half of the issues during any 12-month period); must not be owned by outside business interests; and must not print advertisements free.

To qualify for second class, association and society publications must meet these requirements, except that they do not have to have a paid circulation list if they carry no general advertising. Those carrying advertising must maintain a list, but when members pay for their subscriptions as a part of their dues, no individual subscriptions or receipts are required. It is essential that the bylaws of the organization state specifically that an allocation from dues equivalent to at least 50% of the regular subscription rate is earmarked as a subscription remittance.

To avoid problems, it is advisable to use a membership application form stating, for example: "I apply for membership in _____. Enclosed is $_____ in payment of annual dues for the year _____ including _____ for one year's subscription to (name of magazine)." For each annual renewal: "Enclosed is payment of annual membership dues in _____ in the amount of $_____ of which amount $_____ is for a one year's subscription of (name of magazine)."

Attempts have been made from time to time to establish a principle of "voluntarism." It is argued that the member recipient should have the option of rejecting the magazine at the time he pays his dues, receiving in turn a rebate of the subscription allocation. So far association and society magazines, led by the Society of National Association Publications, have succeeded in persuading the Postal Service not to get involved in this area.

Where to Find the Answers

Direct Mail Manual Sections 422 through 426 include answers to many of the day-to-day problems of magazine publishing. Covered are such subjects as circulation requirements, nominal rate and free circulation, definition of advertising, publications of institutions and societies, controlled circulation, foreign publications, special second-class privileges, and what can be mailed second class such as additions, enclosures, supplements, novelty pages, and special issues.

Identification Statement

The publication must carry an identification statement on one of the first five pages, which must include the publication number (DMM Section 462).

Rates

Rates are carried in the first pages of each class chapter of the DMM. They are too voluminous to reproduce here and are subject to continuing change. Obtain current rates from the local postmaster (DMM Sections 411.2 to 411.38 for second class; Section 611 for third class).

Applications

Application for second-class privileges must be filed before the publication can be mailed at these rates. File Form 3501 with two copies of the issue described in the application at the post office of the place where the publication office is located. Publications of certain institutions and societies file Form 3502. The publication may not be mailed at second-class rates until the Director of the Office of Mail Classification approves the application. Only when the Director has notified the postmaster of approval can it be accepted under second-class rates. Postage under applicable third- or fourth-class rates may be paid under a trust fund arrangement while application is pending. When approved, the applicant will receive the difference between second-class rate and the amount deposited.

Once a publication has obtained second-class entry, it may apply for permission to mail at additional entry post offices. Form 3510 is used for this (see DMM Section 442.1 for details). The Director of Mail Classification rules on all applications and advises the postmaster, who then notifies the applicant. The Director may call the publishers for additional information, and failure to provide such information may result in denial of application.

Ownership Statement

The 39 U.S. Code 3685 requires each owner of a publication having second-class privileges to furnish to the Postmaster General at least once a year and to publish at least once a year information identifying the editor, publisher, owners, stock and security holders, and the extent and nature of the circulation (DMM Section 448). Publishers must file on or before October 1 of each year Form 3526 setting forth such information in duplicate at the office of original entry. Postmasters must furnish publishers at least three copies of Form 3526 10 days before October 1.

Marking Paid Articles

The statutory requirement that newspapers reveal ownership details was one of the first "sunshine laws" enacted by the Congress in the early part of the 20th century to help the press avoid unscrupulous exploitation. Another clause in these laws requires that all paid advertising or other matter for which valuable consideration is paid is marked "advertisement." In 1976 the Postal Service noticed that some scientific magazines were requiring authors to pay for publication of their articles. Invoking the 1912 statute as amended in 1962, the Postal Service threatened withdrawal of second-class privileges unless applicable advertising rates were paid on such material and that it be labeled "advertisement." Through the intervention of a number of scientific journals and the Society of National Association Publications, the Postal Service was persuaded to accept the long-established principle that such payments are necessary to make the proper dissemination of such material economically feasible. It agreed that the law and its regulations would be satisfied if the payment was voluntary on the part of the author and so stated in the magazine. It also agreed to permit marking as "advertisement" only on the first page of any article with the publisher explaining in his masthead pronouncement of the mandatory payment policy that such labeling was merely in technical compliance with 18 U.S. Code 1734.

Cancellation

The Postmaster General may revoke second-class mail privileges when he finds, after a hearing, that the publication no longer is entitled to them. The Director of the Office of Mail Classification makes the determination concerning suspension or revocation subject to appeal and hearing requested by the publisher. The Director upon determination to suspend or revoke notifies the publisher at the last-known office of publication and states the reasons. The ruling is effective in 15 days unless the publisher appeals. A copy of procedures governing appeals may be obtained from the Director, Mail Classification.

Annual Verification

Publishers using second-class mail must maintain records and produce the information on demand, which may be made each year (DMM Section 477). Those having circulation audits by independent auditing bureaus may advise the Director of Mail Classification of such audits (such as those performed by BPA and ABC) and the Director may authorize the postmaster to forego annual verification of those publications for the year verified by the audit bureau (DMM 447.52).

Requester Rule

When controlled circulation was incorporated as a subclass to second-class mail on March 20, 1982, the Postal Service faced the dilemma that involved regarding nonpaid or free circulation as "paid" to conform to the basic premise of second-class regulations. A regulation was developed effective October 1, 1982 requiring a controlled circulation magazine to have 50 percent or more of its circulation paid for by subscription or requested by the reader within the last 3 years to qualify for second-class rates. No detailed regulation to define the procedure has been issued and may not be, leaving interpretation to a case-by-case basis.

Special Nonprofit Rate

Certain periodicals meeting specific criteria may, upon being granted second-class entry, obtain a specific authorization to mail at the special nonprofit rate. To qualify they must fall into one or more of these categories: *a*) religious, *b*) educational, *c*) scientific, *d*) philanthropic, *e*) agricultural, *f*) labor, *g*) veteran, *h*) fraternal (DMM423). Detailed definitions included in this DMM Section should be reviewed carefully.

Many scientific journals qualify for this substantial saving. The definition "scientific" includes this language:

"A nonprofit organization whose primary purpose is one of the following:

1. to conduct research in the applied, pure or natural sciences.

2. to disseminate systemized technical information dealing with applied, pure or natural sciences."

Subscription Fulfillment

Milton C. Paige, Jr.

A definition of subscription fulfillment might be considered as follows: the process by which we convert an order from a subscriber into a label on a publication going to the post office and eventually to the subscriber. This sounds like a reasonably simple procedure, but numerous obstacles along the way can slow down or stop the order before it can be turned into a label.

Before getting into the actual procedure used at the *New England Journal of Medicine (NEJM)*, some background information is in order to help relate problems at other journals to those at the *NEJM* in terms of circulation size, numbers of transactions, and the like.

Until the mid-1940's the circulation was limited to the membership of the Massachusetts Medical Society plus a few thousand independent subscribers attracted by the publication of the Cabot Case Records from the Massachusetts General Hospital. During World War II, the editor arranged with the government to send copies to various service hospitals and installations all over the world. As a result of this tremendous exposure, physicians who had received it at government centers started subscribing independently after the war, and the circulation increased to about 17,000.

Circulation grew slowly for a few years until the early 1950's, when a consistent circulation promotion campaign was started. At that time the subscription list numbered about 25,000. Today it is 210,000 weekly, including 25,000 students, 37,000 interns and residents, and the balance practicing physicians and institutions.

There are three different subscription rates: a regular rate of $48.00 per year for practicing physicians, institutions, libraries, etc.; an intern and resident rate of $35.00; and a student rate of $30.00. Savings are offered on two-and three-year terms for regular subscribers. All rates are higher outside the United States.

Many of the problems in procedures and systems, handling of orders, promotion ideas, and controls are similar for other journals. Differences are mostly in volume. In subscription fulfillment, what must be accomplished? As mentioned before, an order must be converted into a label. Most procedures cannot be defined in categorical terms. As soon as we design a program of rules and regulations, there will be exceptions. For example: "Dear Sir, I'm moving this week, so send my journal to my new address next week." Fine, the only problem is that next week's issue is in the mail and the label for the next week has also been run. Therefore this is not a simple, straightforward change of address. It probably will cause a complaint. Perhaps the journal will be forwarded with postage due, which will irk our subscriber, or perhaps we shall get a couple of "nixies" back from the post office with, we hope, legible forwarding information. Little can be done except to wait for the second shoe to drop.

How do we accomplish the order conversion? What tools of the trade are indicated? The choice depends on three factors: the size of the list, the frequency of publication, and the amount of information needed in the subscriber's record: in other words, the activity of the list.

The *NEJM* keeps records of 210,000 subscribers and mails weekly. For this procedure, they use an in-house IBM System III Model 4331 computer with cathode-ray tubes (CRTs) with on-line file maintenance. The rental for this system is about $120,000 per year. It is a disk-oriented system with a core of 195 K. Each subscriber has a reference number, which is the entry into the computer via the CRT. When the reference number is keyed into the computer, the subscriber's record appears on the screen. Changes are keyed into the visual record and go directly into the computer on completion. This is what is meant by on-line file maintenance. As many as 5000–6000 transactions per week are handled with this system.

In addition to the address information, the subscriber's record includes: term of subscription; billed or paid; type or class (regular, student, intern, resident) for subscription rate; classification (medical doctor, student, institution, exchange, complimentary, etc.); specialty (internist, obstetrician, pediatrician, etc.); society membership; source of order; new subscription or renewed. In addition, a transaction history, five transactions back, is maintained.

With this information keyed into the records, they are able to retrieve accurate statistics necessary for auditing and providing general information, such as accounts receivable and unexpired terms of subscriptions in dollars for the deferred subscription account. This latter account is carried as a liability on the books until the subscription is terminated. Return information on new and renewal promotions is used to ascertain results. Should a change in offer terminology or perhaps a schedule change in the renewal series be tested? Such questions may be raised and there will be a base against which to test or experiment.

Additionally, these print-outs of statistics show the work load by department and operator. They also point out bottlenecks and peaks of work load. For example, from mid-May until mid-July there are usually 4000 to 6000 changes of address per week. There is the capability of keying in changes of address in advance of the effective date so that when the date arrives the change will be made automatically on the computer for the label run involved. June and December are the biggest renewal months; it happens every year. However, any sizable variation in these statistics could mean trouble. Perhaps the renewal mailing schedule was off a few days or postal delivery was worse than usual. Either could cause complaint mail if transactions were received late and not handled quickly. With a weekly publication one cannot wait until tomorrow.

If you are interested only in maintaining a mailing list, with expiry information, to address a few thousand subscriptions monthly or quarterly, obviously you do not need something as sophisticated as a computer. Several relatively simple systems are available for this type of program.

If you are considering a computer for your operation or even if you just wish to determine whether one might be indicated, talk in detail with a publisher who is using one. The manufacturers are reasonably knowledgeable, but a publisher who has been through a systems analysis and programming experience will be much more helpful. Most manufacturers have little or no experience in fulfillment procedures, which means that a journal publisher has to teach them his business first, and that becomes complicated.

The process of subscription fulfillment, or subscriber service, starts with the order of original document. It must first go through what is generally called "caging." The amount of money is circled on the document and the payment is taken out for deposit. Tapes of payments are run and orders are counted before they circulate through the department in batches. About 30 orders make up a batch. Therefore, if an order is misplaced or lost, this will be discovered because the batch count will be off.

About 70% of caging transactions are handled by the bank. A box number is used in the address on the business reply envelopes, which are enclosed with new or renewal promotions. This mail is picked up by the bank and opened; payments are removed and deposited. The bank runs a tape, encloses it with a batch of documents on which amounts have been circled, and forwards it to the *NEJM*. After the accuracy of the tape is checked, the orders go into the mainstream operations. The checking account balance is large enough to obviate an additional charge for this service.

After this procedure, the order is searched and coded. "Searching" means looking up every order that does not have a reference number on it to see if it is a new or renewal transaction. Many renewals are returned on *NEJM*'s promotion material and do not have to be searched. If the subscriber cannot be located on the print-out in zip code order or on the print-out in alphabetical order by name, it is assumed that the number is assigned.

This batch continues on to the CRT operators. There is no separation of new subscriptions and renewals or types of subscriptions, because this batch, after its completed tour through caging, searching, and coding into order entry and the CRT, must always balance out with the original tape from the bank.

The final check on this batch is against the computer print-out statistics of the day's work, which must balance back to the original bank deposit.

The CRT operator is able to spot discrepancies, if there are any, on the order when it appears on the screen. For example, if a payment is received as a renewal and it shows on the screen that the subscriber had already renewed previously, the expiration date is extended without notification. If the subscriber has paid twice and requests a refund, it is sent. It has been found through experience that this is the most efficient way to handle a transaction of this type, and generally the subscriber accepts the extension. The top line or code on the label carries a readable expiry date that many subscribers recognize and watch.

Here is an example of an *NEJM* code line with an explanation of the coded part:

$$0779339 \quad 11/77 \quad 14 \quad 32472$$

The number is the subscriber's personal reference number, i.e., his or her entry into the computer, which will remain unchanged for the duration of the subscription. The second is the expiration date and the third a specialty code.

The last five digits give the issue date and where this particular journal fits in the mailing scheme—whether it is a direct bag, sectional center, or mixed state. If an empty wrapper or "nixie" is returned from the post office, the label will show which copy was missed and it can be replaced. Occasionally a bag of mangled journals and wrappers is returned by the post office with a note to the effect that they were "damaged in handling." The sample above indicates the March 24, 1977 issue. Without this code the journal would have to wait until the customer complained or would have to write to find out which issue was missed.

The key that tells how this particular journal was mailed is the fifth number in the final series. The digit "2" means a sectional center bag. This can prove helpful if a subscriber complains that his journal always arrives damaged or his delivery is inconsistent. The bag and often the route of delivery can be traced. If it is a direct bag to a city zip code, that bag theoretically should not be opened until it arrives at that branch. With accurate information like this, one can generally get action from the post office. Such action may not be easily visible immediately but eventually when the post office officials realize that a publisher is well informed, they are more likely to cooperate. In most cases the post office does try to help.

Complaint mail is processed by the correspondence department. Various forms, designed for quick answers, are used as much as possible. Some forms indicate that the inquiry has been received and the problem is being corrected or that additional information is needed. It is particularly helpful for subscribers to give their personal reference number in any correspondence with the journal.

If there is a serious complaint about service and it appears to be a complicated situation, the subscriber is called on the wide-area telecommunications service (WATS) line. This usually straightens out the problem immediately and also makes the subscriber feel that we really care. In terms of time it is cheaper than writing a letter and then waiting for a reply and taking the chance that something else could happen that might compound the problem further.

Once everything in a batch of orders is checked and balanced, the orders are filed by reference number in folders; a subscriber's complete file can then be pulled to check any question.

Controls similar to those I have mentioned are vital. The basic problem arising in a circulation fulfillment operation is inefficiency: inefficiency of the subscriber, the post office, and the publisher. There must be controls for each facet.

A most important aid in any fulfillment division, regardless of size, is a procedure manual. You should decide what you wish for an end result. Pick the ultimate that you would like to accomplish and start with scheduling and planning to reach this goal. You may well discover that the goal is attainable with a little adjusting and changing here and there. By setting every step down in a manual for reference you can assure consistency in the operation instead of people doing things "their" way. Inconsistency will breed inefficiency.

A problem we all have, and I am afraid always will have, is erratic delivery by the post office. However, things can be done to help speed delivery from your point of entry to various cities, if your list is large enough.

The journal is mailed second class, with newspaper handling. Partly to satisfy postal requirements and partly to facilitate delivery, we designed a bag tag program that is compatible with the label program.

The weight of the issue for the week is estimated from the information available from the production department relative to the number of pages and inserts. The weight is used to ascertain how many journals can be put in a mail bag and stay within postal weight limits; this information is keyed to the computer.

As the journals are wrapped and labels attached, the last label that fills the bag carries a printed signal that mailing personnel recognize; they then close that bag. In sequence there is a tag for this bag indicating its destination and whether it is a direct bag (all one zip code) or is sectional center, mixed state, or miscellaneous. This means that the post office does not have to empty any bags for sorting until they arrive at their destination. If you can possibly sort to this system, it will pay off.

The above system probably helps to cut down damaged copies. Journals are tied in bundles of 20 or so within the bags so the individual copies are not floating around loose. A problem, however, can arise with the top or bottom copy in a given bundle even though each copy is wrapped individually. As postal workers empty bags on conveyors for delivery to a sorting room at the destination post office, the top or bottom copy can get scuffed or torn, particularly if the worker involved does not keep the conveyor reasonably clear.

You can work with customer representatives of the post office where the journals are mailed. They are cooperative and do try to help, particularly when presented with hard facts. For example, if there is a complaint from a subscriber in Detroit that his journal is always late and damaged, check to see how it is mailed. With this information plus routing information from the printer's dispatch department, go to the post office and point out that a damaged copy was in a direct sack that left Minneapolis on Friday, taking a certain route, and had to be in Detroit on Tuesday at the latest. Therefore the branch delivery of the local post office was probably at fault.

The *NEJM* subscribes to a monitoring service that has test names in several sections of the country. The reports of delivery are helpful because they can be used to point out delays or trends to the post office. One complaint is not going to correct anything, but factual reasonable information does help. It is the old story of the squeaking wheel getting the grease.

One further note on distribution: a few years ago we decided to investigate the possibility of printing in England, to determine whether this might expedite delivery to our 8500 European, Near East, and African subscribers. We contracted with a printer and started this project. In spite of somewhat erratic mailing partly because of the printer and partly because of the casual postal system, we were usually able to deliver copies within 2 weeks instead of 8–12. Subscribers were happy and our circulation list increased to over 12,000. We were printing only the editorial material, omitting the 40–50 pages of advertisements that usually resulted in a 64-page issue. After 18 months of this experiment, I was notified one morning by telephone from London that the printer had decided to go out of business in 2 weeks. A quick decision was obviously needed. We decided to print here and try shipping via KLM into Amsterdam for distribution. This system worked extremely well, and our circulation increased to almost 23,000. In most areas the date of delivery was within a few days of the issue date instead of the previous 8–12 weeks late. To publish this way cost about $300.00 a week more than if we had printed the complete journal here and sent it through normal U.S. postal channels.

Promotion for new business and renewal is an integral part of the fulfillment operation. How many renewal notices should be sent? How should they be spaced? When do they stop? Ask publishers and you will get different answers. The only logical way to get an answer is to test and see what works best for you.

For renewal promotion, the *NEJM* uses a series of four consecutive communications. They are straightforward letters telling the subscriber that his subscription is due for renewal and pointing out that if he renews now, service will not be interrupted. An extra month's issue is offered if his payment accompanies the order, thereby making billing unnecessary. This offer increased payments with orders from 40 to 70% of the total.

The first notice is mailed four months before the expiration month. Currently, subscriptions are terminated by month, not week, although the latter program is planned for implementation in the future. The second notice goes out two months before expiration; the third, one month before; and the fourth during the month of expiration. Thus July expires begin getting the series of notices in March. The first three notices are mailed third class and the final one first class.

A major problem confronting the renewal program is payment overlap with the next notice. If someone is slow in returning a payment, invariably the second notice will be in the mail before the record is updated. This situation is impossible to solve completely. However, with fast, efficient updating the incidence can be kept at a controllable level. With our system, a renewal or change of address is updated the day it is received or no later than the next day. Transactions received Monday through Thursday are effective with the issue mailed 2 weeks later. Our publishing day is Thursday. Take the issue of May 19 for example. Updating closed at 4:00 p.m. May 5. Issue statistics were set up and translation done May 6. Labels were run May 9 and shipped May 11, and the journal was in the mail May 13.

The *NEJM* allows a grace period of one month after the expiration month before cutoff. I found through experience that it pays to do this rather than cut people off and then put them back on again and send back copies so they do not lose continuity. Even so, the "reinstate" list is between 500 and 600 per month. This process is time consuming and costly, but so many subscribers bind their journals that we were unable to escape it. Agency payments present the biggest problem because agencies accumulate orders before sending them in. In a batch of several hundred, 15 or 20% may be subject to cutoff even after the grace period. If back copies are not provided, the subscriber complains because he had paid several weeks earlier. Then one faces a three-way correspondence argument, with the journal in the middle. If more than four copies are missed, however, the agency pays the back-copy rate of $1.50 per copy.

The question "What is a good renewal percentage?" is almost impossible to answer. There are so many variables that there is no rule of thumb. The *NEJM* renewal rate is in excess of 87%, perhaps even as high as 91%. It is a very difficult number to pin down despite the results of various circulation audits. Reinstated subscriptions, which expired three or four months before the subscribers sent in payments asking for back copies to maintain their volume continuity, should be considered renewals.

Some of the problems that can arise in the fulfillment department and some of their cures have been discussed in this chapter. It is important to recognize that, if systems are designed to control the exceptions, daily procedures will operate more smoothly. A smooth and efficient operation will also help keep costs down in the most expensive area—the complaint department. This keeps business managers smiling.

Budgeting, Accounting, and Financial Planning

Roy C. Fletcher and John R. Rice

The role of an accountant in an association can be compared to that of a doctor who takes a patient's pulse. Through the various tests and application of approved techniques, he continually measures the financial health of his organization. With the use of budgets, financial report analyses, and sound accounting procedures, he strives to promote the sound financial growth of his organization. This chapter describes some of the tools used, the techniques applied, and some of the pitfalls to avoid.

BUDGETING

Why budget? Is it only because your governing body requires it or is it because it is thought to be an important management tool?

Many organizations go through the exercise of budgeting strictly as a formality required by their council or governing body. They fail to realize that the budget is a financial expression of the projected plans and programs of the organization. Another type of organization overreacts to the importance of a budget. Such an organization tends to use comparison with budget as its sole measure of success or failure. Excessive emphasis on the budget can, however, be as harmful as ignoring the budget, and management should carefully avoid it (1).

BUDGETING TECHNIQUES

A budget is a plan of action. It represents the organization's blueprint for the coming months or years expressed in monetary terms (2). This implies that an organization knows its goals; otherwise it is extremely difficult to plan in a meaningful way.

The first step in planning, then, is to set goals for the coming period. Does the society plan to market a new journal, split off a journal, or publish a new book? The goals should be realistic within the framework of the talent and capability of personnel within the organization; on the other hand it is important not to sell oneself short and, by all means, not to let a conservative accountant scuttle all innovative ideas.

Although budget preparation is normally the role of the controller or financial manager, it is essential to good budgeting that participation and support of the budget programs be vested in the executives and/or department heads responsible for these programs. Program managers cannot be expected to conform to a budget when they did not participate in its formulation. Table 1 presents a typical budget preparation schedule; it is just a sample and can be adjusted to fit the needs of the individual organization. One word of caution about setting up a timetable; if at the task IV level it becomes evident that a dues or subscription price increase will be necessary, the target date scheduled should allow time for the required approval procedure. Otherwise the level of income to support the desired program expenditures may not be attainable during the period being planned. This could delay programs or require use of available reserves.

Budget participation can be made more effective by the careful design of standard input forms and the use of budget meetings at the various levels of responsibility. Forms used in collecting budget data should be in the format of the accounting chart of accounts and the existing accounting system. Comparison of actual results to the budget is difficult if the budget and accounting systems differ in basic format (1).

Accounting systems and budget formats will vary widely from organization to

TABLE 1. Flow chart: budget preparation plan

Task	Target Date	Responsibility	June	July	Aug	Sept	Oct	Nov	Dec
I. Prepare preliminary description of programs or goals for coming year (a) Objectives (b) Advantages/disadvantages (c) Personnel requirements (d) Cost estimates	July 1	Department heads							
II. Prepare first draft of department budget	Aug 1	Department heads and Controller							
III. Prepare income budget and assemble expense budget	Sept 1	Controller							
IV. Review of first draft	Sept 15	Executive staff							
V. Review of staff-approved first draft	Oct 1	Finance/Budget Committee							
VI. Revision as required	Oct 15	Executive staff							
VII. Presentation to Board of Directors and/or Council	Nov 1	Treasurer, Exec. Director, Controller							

TABLE 2.   Expense budgeting by journal

Expense	Journal A	Journal B	Journal C	Total Journals
Direct expenses				
Text manufacturing	$175,000	$50,000	$100,000	$325,000
Advertising	7,000	1,000	2,000	10,000
Reprints	30,000	10,000	20,000	60,000
Back volumes	4,000	1,000	3,000	8,000
Office of Editor	10,000	5,000	7,000	22,000
Total direct expenses	$226,000	$67,000	$132,000	$425,000
Allocated departments				
Executive	6,000	2,000	4,000	12,000
Managing Editor	11,000	7,000	10,000	28,000
Administration	8,000	3,000	5,000	16,000
Total allocated	$25,000	$12,000	$19,000	$56,000
Total direct and allocated expenses	$251,000	$79,000	$151,000	$481,000

organization, but the resulting financial reports, if properly prepared, should provide a summary of the financial status and the operating results. The financial reports are key elements in portraying the financial strengths or weaknesses of the organization and the resulting gains or losses from its operations.

In the publication program of the American Society for Microbiology, each journal or book is budgeted for and accounted for individually as a separate and distinct program. Tables 2 and 3 illustrate budget alignment of direct publication expenses as well as allocated departmental expenses. The compilation of all income and expenses by journal gives a complete picture of each journal as a "stand alone" operation. Its financial worth as an individual journal and its contribution to the total publication operation can then be measured. In an organization with multiple journals, there quite often will be a mixture of winners and losers, but if a proper balance is maintained, the total operation can be financially sound and the scientific contribution maximized.

What about the income side of budgeting? In many operations, this is the most difficult aspect of the budgeting process. Calculating the member dues, the journal subscriptions, number of book sales, etc. can at times stretch the term "educated guess." The best available guide is history, i.e., what has been the experienced growth of membership, how have subscription sales developed, or what has been the market acceptance of XYZ book? For the development of this information, the two key personnel are the managing editor (or equivalent responsible person on the editorial or "product" side) and the controller. The controller can develop and analyze the historical data while the managing editor projects this information into future potential. This budget, like the expense budget, can be prepared on an individual journal basis (Table 4).

TABLE 3. Expense budgeting for allocated departments

Expenses	Executive	Managing Editor	Administrative	Totals
Salaries and wages	$60,000	$75,000	$50,000	$185,000
Salary-related expenses	12,000	15,000	10,000	37,000
Temporary help	2,000	5,000	2,000	9,000
Printing and duplicating	2,000	3,000	3,000	8,000
Telephone and telegraph	2,000	2,000	2,000	6,000
Office supplies	4,000	6,000	5,000	15,000
Postage	2,000	5,000	4,000	11,000
Insurance	1,000	1,000	1,000	3,000
Occupancy costs	5,000	8,000	5,000	18,000
Travel and entertainment	5,000	3,000	2,000	10,000
Data processing			5,000	5,000
Depreciation: office equipment	1,000	2,000	2,000	5,000
Miscellaneous	1,000	1,000	1,000	3,000
Total allocation expense	$97,000	$126,000	$92,000	$315,000
Basis for allocation	Direct Cost	Text pages	Direct Cost	

The income budget combined with the expense budget gives a projection of financial operations for each journal as shown in Table 5.

Once this detailed information is available, one can then proceed to summarize information for all journals into total income and expenses by types, e.g., total member subscription income and total text manufacturing expense.

This information in the preliminary stage of budgeting can help answer many haunting questions—do you need to increase member and nonmember subscription rates or must you delay that new program for lack of sufficient income?

BUDGET REVISIONS

Can budgets be changed or revised? Yes. Should budgets be changed or re-

TABLE 4. Income budgeting by journal

Expense	Journal A	Journal B	Journal C	Total Journals
Subscriptions: member	$100,000	$20,000	$60,000	$180,000
Subscriptions: nonmember	50,000	10,000	25,000	85,000
Advertising	15,000	2,000	4,000	21,000
Reprints	65,000	20,000	40,000	125,000
Back volume and late renewals	7,000	2,000	2,000	11,000
Page charge	25,000	10,000	20,000	55,000
Manuscript handling	10,000	5,000	10,000	25,000
Total income	$272,000	$69,000	$161,000	$502,000

TABLE 5. Journal operating budget

	Income	Expense
Journal A		
Subscriptions: member	$100,000	$ —
Subscriptions: nonmember	50,000	—
Text manufacturing	—	175,000
Advertising	15,000	7,000
Reprints	65,000	30,000
Back volume and late renewals	7,000	4,000
Page charge	25,000	—
Manuscript handling	10,000	—
Office of Editors	—	10,000
Allocations: Executive	—	6,000
Managing Editor	—	11,000
Administrative	—	8,000
Total Journal A (net income $21,000)	$272,000	$251,000

vised? Perhaps. During the budgeting period, conditions may arise that warrant a revision of the budget. However, budget revisions should be (and *should be* is emphasized) limited to those instances where major changes in income or expense develop.

All too often, when a comparison of actual to budget figures shows a trend of escalating expense, the only solution offered is "revise the budget." A budget that is changed or revised too often loses the continuity necessary for orderly planning. Budget revisions should be considered only after a thorough review of all other possibilities such as curtailment of planned programs, special assessments, or other offsetting alternatives.

CASH FLOW BUDGETING

"Bankruptcy" may seem a harsh and remote word to many, but in the past few years many organizations have become very familiar with its consequences. The importance or reputation of an organization will not of itself protect it. As Malvern J. Gross, Jr. stated in his book, *Financial and Accounting Guide for Nonprofit Organizations*: "While it might seem like a simple task to recognize that the organization is in, or is headed for financial trouble, the fact is that many organizations hide their heads in the sand like ostriches and fail to recognize the symptoms at the time when they might be able to do something" (2). Avoiding bankruptcy takes effort and skill.

The cash flow budget is another key ingredient in obtaining a complete picture of the organization's activities. Many transactions, while not directly affecting income and expense under an accrual accounting system, do affect the available cash. Some of these transactions are borrowing money, repayment of loans, inventory buildup, and equipment purchases. These transactions, combined with cash transac-

TABLE 6. Cash flow budget

Description	January	February	March	October	November	December	Year 1980
Beginning cash balance	$50,000	$74,000	$94,000	$12,000	$25,000	$5,000	$50,000
Add receipts							
Subscriptions	100,000	90,000	50,000	80,000	110,000	140,000	930,000
Accounts receivable collections	30,000	45,000	10,000	40,000	35,000	30,000	310,000
Dues	20,000	10,000	5,000	20,000	25,000	40,000	250,000
Meetings registration	5,000	—	10,000	10,000	5,000	10,000	170,000
Other cash receipts	10,000	5,000	5,000	10,000	5,000	10,000	90,000
Total receipts	165,000	150,000	80,000	160,000	180,000	230,000	1,750,000
Less disbursements							
Payroll and related expenses	30,000	30,000	30,000	30,000	30,000	30,000	390,000
Accounts payable	100,000	90,000	110,000	100,000	110,000	100,000	1,200,000
Other miscellaneous disbursements	10,000	10,000	20,000	15,000	10,000	10,000	150,000
Total disbursements	140,000	130,000	160,000	145,000	150,000	140,000	1,740,000
Net balance after operations	75,000	94,000	14,000	27,000	55,000	95,000	60,000
Add receipts of sales from maturing investments	—	—	100,000	—	—	—	100,000
Deduct loan repayment	—	—	—	—	50,000	50,000	100,000
Equipment purchase	1,000	—	5,000	2,000	—	5,000	20,000
Investment purchase	—	—	100,000	—	—	—	100,000
Net cash balance	74,000	94,000	9,000	25,000	5,000	40,000	(60,000)
Borrowings	—	—	—	—	—	—	100,000
Ending cash balance	$74,000	$94,000	$9,000	$25,000	$5,000	$40,000	$40,000

tions resulting from the operations budget, will provide the cash flow budget required to provide complete cash control. Table 6 shows a sample cash flow budget.

Even with this cash flow budget showing adequate cash balances at the end of each month, it is of little value if there is likely to be insufficient cash at points during the month. This is a point the controller or financial manager should watch closely, especially when major payments such as bank loan repayments or taxes fall at midmonth dates.

ACCOUNTING: CASH VERSUS ACCRUAL

Cash basis accounting has been used for many years by associations. It has a principal advantage of being simple for people who are not accountants to understand and to use in keeping records. By this method the executive sees what the weekly income and disbursements are just as they familiarly appear in his household financial records. For some associations, the difference between results on a cash basis and an accrual basis may not be materially different, and they therefore conclude that the cash method is adequate.

However, the users of the cash method should be ever vigilant against the possibly misleading results that this method can produce. Just because cash has been received does not always imply that income has been earned from an accounting standpoint. Take, for instance, the journal subscriptions, prepaid at the beginning of the year, whose acceptance requires fulfillment services throughout the year. Under the cash method, income from the subscription would be reported in full, but expense would not be accounted for until the journal or journals were produced. Many associations have found that the cash method does not portray all the information necessary for sound appraisal of their financial operations or status.

The accrual method of accounting is today widely accepted as providing the complete record of all transactions of an organization for any given period of time. In a Statement of Position (78-10) issued by the Accounting Standards Division, American Institute of Certified Public Accounts (AICPA), on December 31, 1978, accrual accounting was adopted as a requirement for use by nonprofit organizations (3).

The basic attribute of accrual accounting is that it matches income and expense in the period to which the transaction relates, regardless of the period in which cash was disbursed or received. This permits accurate accounting of income earned and expenses incurred and the preparation of meaningful financial statements. For these reasons, most organizations will find accrual basis accounting not only preferable but essential.

THE ACCOUNTING SYSTEM

To use the accrual basis, an accounting system is required that can provide for separation of prepaid expenses, inventories, accounts receivable, accounts payable, deferred income, and the many other items related to accrual accounting. Thus we should be familiar with the following accounting terms and definitions as they may relate to publications.

• *Accounts receivable*—Sale of a product or service for which payment has not been made. This usually is the result of an invoice being rendered for an item, such as a book sale, for which payment will be forthcoming.

• *Prepaid expenses*—Expenses paid in advance of their being needed or used. Universities may require payment for a journal editor's supplies, postage, and secretarial services in advance of the period of time in which they are expended.

• *Inventories*—Value of unused or salable items having material value. A prime example would be books published and held for future sales.

• *Accounts Payable*—Services or goods purchased but not paid for, such as the invoice just received from the printer of a journal.

• *Deferred income*—The value of payment received for some future services. Subscription payments received at the end of the current year, but relating to the supply of journals for the coming year, are deferred until earned or journals are delivered.

All of the above are termed balance sheet accounts and their proper use is an integral part of accrual accounting. The important matching of income and expense can now be accomplished even though the expense transaction may be separated by months or years from the income transaction or vice versa.

BUDGET VERSUS ACTUAL RESULTS

Now that there is a budget and an accounting system capable of recording all transactions, the next logical step is the comparison of actual results with the previously documented "plan of action." Management should be provided periodic comparisons with any substantial variances analyzed. What should be done about the variances depends upon the nature and cause of each.

It should be noted that operating results conforming exactly to the budget are the exception, not the rule. Budget variances are routine occurrences, and a good manager exercises his skill by analyzing and reacting to them (1).

If, based upon the analysis, the variances are found to result from inaccurate assumptions, the basis for arriving at these assumptions should be changed to provide more accurate projections for future planning. If inefficiency or disregard for budget constraint is the cause of variance, the problem is then centered around the performance of the operating personnel.

A manager who has successfully determined the cause of variance must next decide what to do about the consequences of the variance. If the variance is one of less income or greater expense with no offsetting increase in income, then the organization is faced with several choices. The first could be to continue by using existing reserves, a second could be to reduce future expenses, a third could to be increase future income.

As mentioned before, variance is a routine occurrence and of itself may not be a reason to cut back activity in another area. Minor value variance can be handled through reserves, but major or continuing variances should alert management for action that may include major changes in the way operations are handled (1).

The process of comparing the actual results with the budget is extremely important. If adhered to carefully, serious depressions in operating results can be avoided and future revenue requirements can be planned far enough in advance to avoid emergency increases to members.

FEDERAL TAX REQUIREMENTS

The Internal Revenue Code provides tax exemption for certain types of organizations (4). The most common types having this exemption are listed below.

• 501(c)(2) Corporations organized for the exclusive purpose of holding title to property, collecting income therefrom, and turning over the entire amount thereof, less expenses, to an organization which is itself exempt under this section.

• 501(c)(3) Corporations, and any community chest, fund, or foundation, organized and operated exclusively for religious, charitable, scientific, testing for public safety, literary, or educational purposes . . . no substantial part of the activities of which is carrying on propaganda, or otherwise attempting to influence legislation and which does not participate in, or intervene in (including the publishing or distributing of statements), any political campaign on behalf of any candidate for public office.

• 501(c)(6) Business leagues, chambers of commerce, real estate boards, boards of trade, or professional football leagues . . . not organized for profit and no part of the net earnings of which inures to the benefit of any private shareholder or individual.

• 501(c)(7) Clubs organized for pleasure, recreation, and other nonprofitable purposes, substantially all of the activities of which are for such purposes and no part of the net earnings of which inures to the benefit of any private shareholder.

There are other exempt classifications, but those listed above are the primary ones applicable to nonprofit organizations.

Amost all tax-exempt organizations are required to file an annual information return, Form 990, "Return of Organizations Exempt from Income Tax." It includes general information on income, contributions, disbursements, assets and liabilities, and the names and addresses of substantial contributors. This information return must be filed by the 15th day of the fifth month after the end of the organization's fiscal year. For instance, the due date for a calendar year organization would be May 15.

In addition to this information return, any organization having unrelated business income of $1000 or more must file a separate tax return, Form 990-T, and pay taxes at the regular corporate rate on all taxable income in excess of the $1000 specific deduction.

UNRELATED BUSINESS INCOME

The Internal Revenue Code (4) defines unrelated business income in section 513(a) as "any trade or business the conduct of which is not substantially related . . . to the exercise or performance by such organization of its charitable, educational, or other purpose of functions constituting the basis for its exemption. . . ."

A major source of unrelated business income for many organizations results from advertising. Although it was argued that advertising helps support the cost of publication, which itself may be an exempt function, advertising has been ruled to be unrelated business income. The fact that the activity helps pay for the exempt function is not enough, but must be in itself part of the exempt function. It is true that production of advertising income has associated expenses that are allowable deductions when they are directly connected with the income. However, this regulation does place the burden on the organization of keeping its records in a manner that will substantiate the claimed deductions.

In addition to the direct advertising expenses, an organization may also offset losses from its publication operation not connected with advertising against the net gain from advertising sales. This calculation of taxable unrelated business income is given in Table 7.

In the examples in Table 7, the first step was to determine net gain or loss from direct advertising. At this level, only expenses directly related to advertising are allowable deductions. The type of costs that can be deducted depends on your organization's involvement in the advertising business. Generally they include such costs as advertising copy and manufacturing costs, advertising sales commissions, and similiar expenses. Also allowable would be allocated expenses (overhead) within the prescribed limitations set forth by the Code. Step 2 is a calculation of gain or loss from all journal activity exclusive of unrelated advertising. These are income and expenses related to the exempt activities of the organization. Step 3 is a combination of steps 1 and 2 and shows the consolidated gain or loss of each entry.

As demonstrated by the examples shown, if circulation income exceeds readership costs (step 2), the taxable unrelated business income is the excess of gross advertising income over direct advertising costs. However, if at the step 2 level a loss is incurred, the taxable unrelated business income is the excess of the net gain attributable to advertising (step 1) less the loss in step 2. A loss must be sustained at the step 1 level to qualify for loss carryover or carryback as demonstrated in example 2, Table 7.

Organizations whose membership dues include the right to receive a periodical can no longer attribute arbitrarily a portion of the dues to the periodical. Internal Revenue Service regulation 1.512(a)lf4i-iii has now clearly dictated rules that exempt organizations should follow in allocating membership receipts.

It is very important that the management of any exempt organization be fully aware of this provision because it could have serious tax implications for those affected. The regulation basically provides that the nonmember subscription price should be used as the periodical price if 20% or more of the total circulation consists of sales to nonmembers. If nonmember subscriptions account for less than 20% of total circulation, then a member subscription price or a prorated allocation of membership receipts based on the relation of periodical costs to other exempt costs must be used.

Other types of income are considered as unrelated business income, such as income derived from the sale or rental of membership lists and debt-financed business property, but advertising is by far the most sizable and affects the most organizations.

CONCLUSION

Accounting for nonprofit organizations is presently undergoing some revolutionary changes because of the ever-increasing role that nonprofit organizations are playing in the economic community. With this new role comes an even greater demand for financial reporting. As a result, more elaborate and sophisticated accounting systems will be required than ever before.

In the past, it was difficult to select or determine the appropriate accounting

TABLE 7.   Unrelated business income: advertising

	Example 1	Example 2	Example 3	Example 4
Step 1				
Gross advertising income	$50,000	$50,000	$50,000	$50,000
Direct advertising costs	25,000	60,000	30,000	30,000
Net gain (loss) attributable to advertising	$25,000	$(10,000)	$20,000	$20,000
Step 2				
Circulation income	$75,000		$100,000	$90,000
Readership costs	125,000	N/A	90,000	100,000
Net gain (loss)	$(50,000)		$10,000	$(10,000)
Step 3				
Total income	$125,000		$150,000	$140,000
Total costs	150,000	N/A	120,000	130,000
Net gain (loss)	$(25,000)		$30,000	$10,000
Taxable unrelated business income from advertising	$ —	$(10,000)*	$20,000	$10,000

*Qualifies for loss carryover or carryback.

principles for tax-exempt organizations. Although accountants, especially those associated with publication operations, followed commercial-type accounting principles, there were no established accounting principles for those in organizations in the not-for-profit area.

The Accounting Standards Division of the AICPA prepared a Statement of Position (78-10) on Accounting Principles and Reporting Practices for Certain Nonprofit Organizations dated December 31,1978 (3). This statement was later adopted by the Financial Accounting Standards Board and represents the state of the art in accounting reporting for tax-exempt organizations. This statement of position applies to all nonprofit organizations not covered by previously issued AICPA industry audit guidelines that cover hospitals, colleges and universities, voluntary health and welfare organizations, and state and local government units.

The major points adopted by the AICPA that affect accounting for journal operations are listed below:

• Financial statements of nonprofit organizations must be prepared using the accrual basis of accounting to conform with generally accepted accounting principles.

• Fund accounting (classification of resources into funds associated with specified activities or objectives) is highly recommended where there is a need to segregate unrestricted from restricted resources.

• The statement of activity (revenue and expenses) should present figures separately for each significant program and supporting activity rather than summarize amounts using natural classifications (i.e., salaries, printing). Both methods can be satisfied on a columnar schedule showing revenue and expenses being spread to the various journals and other projects conducted by the organizaton.

• Financial statements of the current period should be presented on a comparative basis with figures from financial statements for one or more prior reporting periods.

• Donated or voluntary services need not be reported as support and expense unless certain circumstances exist (i.e., services are required and would otherwise be performed by salaried employee; organization controls employment and duties of volunteer; there is a measurable basis for amount to be recorded).

• Depreciation accounting is required (distribution of cost or other basic value of tangible capital assets, less salvage, if any, over estimated useful life).

The requirements under the Statement of Position became effective with fiscal years beginning after December 31, 1980.

Whether an organization is large or small, a good accounting system is essential for good management. On the other hand, the best accounting system ever devised is of little value unless it is used to facilitate control and disclosure. The foundations of a financially sound organization are a good accounting system, effective budgeting, timely reporting, and a management willing to take corrective action when necessary.

REFERENCES

1. Harris, A. F. M. Association accounting. Washington, DC: Touche Ross & Co.; 1976; 18.07.
2. Gross, M. J., Jr. Financial and accounting guide for nonprofit organizations. New York, NY: The Ronald Press Co.; 1972.
3. Statement of Position (78-10): Accounting principles and reporting practices for certain nonprofit organizations. New York, NY: Accounting Standards Division, American Institute of Certified Public Accountants; December 31, 1978.
4. Complete Internal Revenue Code of 1954. Englewood Cliffs, NJ: Prentice-Hall Inc.; June 1, 1978.

Marketing the Scientific Journal

Morna Conway Schmick

The term "marketing" is sometimes used in the narrow sense of advertising and sales promotion. These are, however, only *tools* of the marketing effort, which in its full sense starts with a product, or an idea for a product, and ends with that product producing a profit (or loss) for its owner. The marketing process involves product knowledge; appropriate pricing for the product, in light of costs, competition, and projected profitability; knowledge of the potential customer and how many potential customers exist (marketplace); knowledge of how to sell the product to its potential marketplace (sales, advertising, sales promotion); how to get the product into the customers' hands (distribution) and how to follow up on the sale, either in terms of service or repeat or related business.

This chapter does not discuss in detail the creation of the editorial product, the journal's design, its manufacture, or its pricing. The following comments touch on these only insofar as they relate to marketing. In the scientific journal field, and particularly with society or association publications, journals exist because editorially there is a need for them. New journals are discussed later in terms of market research, but there is usually (or should be) a good reason for their appearance. In general we may view the design or *packaging* of a journal as a minor consideration in the marketing process, in marked contrast to commercial packaging, where a product can be merchandised soley on the basis of its presentation to the public. However, in the planning of journal *manufacture,* contributors, readers, and others must be considered. High-magnification electron micrographs, for example, should be printed on top-grade coated stock: otherwise, potential contributors may publish elsewhere. Trim size and advertising placement policies, too, are important to the potential advertiser. The scientific journal is less prone to consumer rejection on the basis of price than many other products, probably because of the subscriber's need for it. With an established journal, price increases are expected to keep pace with general inflationary trends in the economy, and the subscriber will balk only at what seem to be unwarranted jumps in price. If the subscription rate is raised directly from, say, $25.00 to $40.00, cancellations may be expected unless there is an accompanying increase in service to the subscriber. Establishing subscription rates in the first place must be accomplished by projecting income and expense.

This chapter discusses the essential features important in the marketing of sci-

entific journals, the strategies that will deliver a journal to its potential audience, namely:
- defining new sources of subscribers for the established journal,
- promoting the scientific journal to new audiences,
- launching a new journal,
- renewal strategies,
- cost-effective methods of promotional techniques.

DEFINING NEW SOURCES OF SUBSCRIBERS

The defining of new sources of subscribers for an established journal is accomplished by three procedures:

1) analyzing present circulation and comparing the present figures with those of previous years;

2) comparing circulation figures with the total numbers of "potential" subscribers;

3) evaluating possible untapped audiences for the journal.

For scientific journals, the most common demographic breakdowns of circulation are as follows:
- member/nonmember
- nonmember individual/nonmember institution
- domestic/foreign.

Further refinements of demographics include, for individual subscribers, occupation or scientific discipline, how many years a subscriber, age, sex; and for institutional subscribers, type of library—hospital, government, university, etc. The first set of criteria is generally available by analyzing the subscription records or mailing tape. The second, more sophisticated set of data is usually obtained by questionnaires sent out to new subscribers or with renewal bills; the answers are then recorded and stored, ready for statistical compilation on the whole subscription file. Apart from providing invaluable marketing information, the more sophisticated demographic data are essential to the advertising sales effort.

The purpose of comparing the present with the past is, of course, to help in evaluating changing trends in the journal's circulation. For example, if fewer members are subscribing to a journal now than in 1981 but the membership has not de-

TABLE 1.   Demographic data for a hypothetical journal

		1982 Circulation	Totals
Member subscriptions	Domestic	2200	2300
	Foreign	100	
Nonmember individual	Domestic	500	500
	Foreign	—	
Nonmember libraries	Domestic	400	600
	Foreign	200	
Total circulation			3400

TABLE 2. Circulation comparisons for hypothetical journal

		5-Year Comparison				
		1982	1981	1980	1979	1978
Member	Domestic	2200	2200	2400	2100	2000
	Foreign	100	200	200	100	100
Nonmember individual	Domestic	500	400	600	600	600
	Foreign	—	—	—	—	—
Libraries	Domestic	400	400	500	500	400
	Foreign	200	200	200	200	200
Totals		3400	3400	3900	3500	3300

clined, it is important to determine *why* there has been a drop. It is only by performing this kind of evaluation that one can decide what, if anything, to do.

Again, as part of the evaluation process, it is essential to compare what circulation *is* with what it *could be*. Suppose a journal is directed primarily toward practicing pediatricians. Its combined domestic member and nonmember individual circulation is 7000. A total of 28,000 members of the American Medical Association define themselves as pediatricians. At first glance, it appears that the journal has good growth potential, since it has only one-third penetration in its primary marketplace. Establishing a "reasonable" market penetration for a particular journal calls for in-depth knowledge of the particular journal and its marketplace, in addition to trend extrapolation on circulation over a number of years. It is very unlikely that 100% penetration is an attainable goal for any journal, but the more focused the editorial content and the more targeted the definition of the marketplace, the higher the potential market penetration.

The third category, defining untapped audiences, is the most hazardous for the marketing person. For example, the foreign circulation of a journal may be minuscule, yet its editors believe it has sales potential overseas. No promotion has ever been done outside the United States. There is, in other words, insufficient evidence to come to any valid conclusion. What should be done? Or the editor may notice that the kinds of articles being cited in the journal have changed radically over the last five years, and the periodical has changed from being predominantly a "rat" journal to being now a predominantly "human" journal. The demographic data show that over a five-year period member subscriptions have declined by 15%, but nonmember individual subscriptions have increased. Furthermore, the new subscribers are describing themselves as medical doctors, with cardiology as a primary specialty. Still, there are only 300 of them, a small percentage of the 10,000 cardiologist members of the American Medical Association. What should the editors do? In relation to this question, Tables 1–3 show demographic data and potential markets for a typical (hypothetical) journal published by a hypothetical society. Even without more sophisticated demographic breakdowns, at this point one can ask some informed questions and come up with some possible courses of action. For example, why has total circulation declined since 1980? Is the overall world economy the culprit? Was there a change in editorial direction? Did the subscription fulfillment pro-

TABLE 3.   Projected circulation for hypothetical journal

	Potential Audience		
	Domestic	Foreign	Combined
Member (actual number)	4,000	500	4,500
Nonmember individual (1)	6,000	3,000	9,000
Nonmember individual (2)	8,000	5,000	13,000
Nonmember individual (3)	2,000	1,000	3,000
Libraries	1,000	1,500	2,500
Totals	21,000	11,000	32,000

cess break down? Have there been out-of-line price increases? How long ago, if ever, was an active campaign to solicit new subscribers launched? Why does only half of the membership subscribe to "their" journal? For a hypothetical journal, these questions cannot, of course, be answered, but the tables and questions are offered as guidelines for all who are involved in circulation development. Also, the following two points should always be kept in mind:

• It is axiomatic that marketing analysis is performed as a preliminary to *selling* new subscriptions.

• Without facts, it is impossible to do any meaningful marketing analysis, and therefore it is essential that the journal's manager collect, on an ongoing basis, data about the journal's circulation.

PROMOTING THE ESTABLISHED JOURNAL TO NEW AUDIENCES

Any audience may be defined as "new" if it has not been solicited for subscriptions within the last year, for the current volume. If a journal subscription is not automatically part of society dues, the membership is a new audience whenever it has not recently been canvassed for subscription to your journal. The library marketplace likewise may have been neglected as a "new" audience.

Assuming that the results of the marketing analysis suggest that there is growth potential in the member, nonmember individual, and institutional markets, how can subscriptions be sold most effectively to these groups? Undoubtedly the most effective sales approach is personal selling. However, with the cost of a sales call these days averaging $100.00, it is obviously not cost-effective to plan on calling personally on every librarian, or every practicing pediatrician, in the hope of selling subscriptions. The only effective, and cost-effective, substitute is *direct mail*, which incorporates the salient features of personal selling—a personal message, delivered to a specific person, with a convenient method of ordering the product—and which costs, on average, 40 cents per message delivered. The beauty of direct mail as a marketing tool is that its results can be objectively measured. Just as we need hard facts to analyze the marketplace, we need hard facts to measure the results of the marketing effort. Another positive feature of direct mail is that it permits its users to *test* markets, while simultaneously selling the journal. Thus direct mail is used not only to sell subscriptions but to generate data for further marketing efforts.

For the *Hypothetical Journal,* how would we construct a direct mail promotion package to generate subscriptions from the potential audience of 32,000? If we assume that fairly reliable information about the journal has been obtained from its manager and are convinced that the decline in subscriptions since 1980 was basically due to a combination of the world recession and the absence of promotion since 1979, we decide that a promotion to domestic and foreign members and libraries is in order. However, we have some hesitation about the nonmember individual sales potential. We have identified 25,000 potential subscribers in three occupational categories, but the journal currently has only 500 nonmember individual subscribers. To mail to the entire 25,000 would cost about $10,000.00. We have no evidence that the mailing would result in significant sales. We would therefore use direct mail to test, using a random sampling technique, say 10% or 2500 of the potential audience. If the test results indicate that a mailing to the total would be worthwhile, then one could go to the entire group. Thus a marketing plan for the *Hypothetical Journal* might appear as follows:

Direct mail: letter + brochure + order form in no. 10 envelope

Lists: Total membership
      10% nonmember individual (1)
      10% nonmember individual (2)   Domestic + foreign
      10% nonmember individual (3)
      Total libraries

Coding: Each list is coded on the label or on the order form, so that we know which list generated what percentage response and dollar volume.

The mailing goes out, the results are tabulated over a two- to three-month period (longer for foreign, sent surface mail), and we now have some new data for future planning. Table 4 codifies the results, assuming a $20.00 member subscription, and a $40.00 nonmember subscription rate.

From the above data, we are now in a position to draw certain fundamental conclusions about the *Hypothetical Journal's* marketplace and how to pursue new subscribers.

• The cost-effective lists are domestic members, nonmember individual (1) domestic and foreign, and nonmember individual (3) domestic and foreign.

• The library mailings, domestic and foreign, are the least cost-effective in terms of direct response. However, before leaping to conclusions about disastrous library mailings, a quick check is made of nonmember institutional circulation, comparing figures at a comparable time over the last few years, and counting the numbers of library subscriptions. We find that, in fact, we have just added 50 new domestic library subscriptions, and 30 new foreign. Remember that the figures given above are *directly traceable* to the promotion, i.e., they are received on order forms.

TABLE 4.   Results from a test promotional mailing

List		Quantity	No. Traceable Responses	% Response	$ Volume	Cost per Piece	Total Cost	Cost per $ Sales
Member	Domestic	4000	200	5%	$4000	$0.40	$1600	$0.40
	Foreign	500	10	2	200	0.50	250	1.75
Nonmember individual	Domestic	600	60	10	2400	0.45	270	0.11
(1)	Foreign	300	15	5	600	0.55	165	0.27
Nonmember individual	Domestic	800	8	1	320	0.45	360	1.12
(2)	Foreign	500	5	1	200	0.55	275	1.37
Nonmember individual	Domestic	200	4	2	160	0.45	90	0.56
(3)	Foreign	100	2	2	80	0.55	55	0.68
Library	Domestic	1000	3	0.3	120	0.40	400	3.33
	Foreign	1500	3	0.2	120	0.50	750	6.25

Librarians generally do not respond directly to direct mail. Rather than using the journal's order form, they subscribe through subscription agents or send in a purchase order. Therefore the effectiveness of the institutional promotion can only be measured in terms of overall growth in library subscriptions.

• The other lists tested were not particularly spectacular in producing sales nor were they cost-effective. However, a case could be made for continuing to promote to these lists, because all of them would become cost-effective if the renewal factor (assuming they renew for 3–5 years) were taken into consideration.

Table 5 shows the projection of a mailing to the entire marketplace and its results, using an average cost of $400.00/M for domestic and $500.00/M for foreign subscribers, the cost variations caused by testing various lists having been wiped out.

This is the dynamic end result of sound marketing analysis, combined with a solid approach to promotion by direct mail. Will such an approach work for your journal? By going through the steps outlined here, you will have sufficient informa-

TABLE 5.   Projection of a promotional mailing to the entire marketplace

List		Quantity	No. New Subscribers	$ Volume	Cost
Member	Domestic	4,000	200	$4,000	$1,600
	Foreign	500	10	200	250
Nonmember individual (1)	Domestic	6,000	600	24,000	2,400
	Foreign	3,000	150	6,000	1,500
Nonmember individual (2)	Domestic	8,000	80	3,200	3,200
	Foreign	5,000	50	2,000	2,500
Nonmember individual (3)	Domestic	2,000	40	1,600	800
	Foreign	1,000	20	800	500
Library	Domestic	1,000	50	2,000	400
	Foreign	1,500	30	1,200	750
Totals		32,000	1230	$45,000	$13,900

tion to make informed decisions about this and the marketing strategy for your journal.

LAUNCHING A NEW JOURNAL

If a society is planning to publish a brand new journal, perhaps as a spin-off from an established journal, perhaps as the society's first journal, perhaps as a new vehicle in a rapidly growing field, much thought must be given to the editorial concept and planned content, the packaging or design, the manufacturing, and the pricing. In preliminary budgeting, for example, it is obviously essential to have an idea of promotional costs and projected subscription income before one can arrive at a list price. However, if at all possible, fairly extensive market research should be performed *before* any final commitment to publish is made and *before* any budget is drawn. Too many journals launched without such a study have either folded quickly or never met the publisher's expectation of sales or budget. Most publishers, however, are either unwilling or unable to conduct extensive market research. It is one thing to say we shall reach 15% of our primary target market in the first year and quite another to prove that statement before the fact, when one has nothing but "gut" feeling about the potential for the new journal. In marketing there can be no hard and fast rules, no convenient formulas because every product is unique. We can discuss averages and probabilities ad infinitum, but only facts are real, and all the wishing in the world will not alter circulation figures or make predictions come true.

If a society is committed to launch a new journal but has no budget for market research, how should one go about selling subscriptions to this unknown entity? There are not even sample copies or a firm table of contents for the first issue. The following are suggested techniques.

• With any new product, whether it is an automobile or a scientific journal, the marketing strategy develops from defining the *unique selling proposition.* Why is this journal being published? How does it differ from existing journals? Why should a person subscribe to it? What will it do for its readers? Suitable promotional copy based on the answers to these questions is extremely important in the selling of new journals.

• For a journal, as for other products, you define the potential market, again using the kind of demographic matrix we developed for an established journal. Assuming that a journal subscription is not part of member dues, we might arrive at the following profile.

Audience	*Quantity*
Members	20,000
Libraries	4,000
Nonmember individual (1)	12,000
Nonmember individual (2)	33,000
Nonmember individual (3)	17,000
Nonmember individual (4)	5,000
Total potential audience	91,000

With a new journal, every conceivable source of subscribers (but not, in desperation, inconceivable ones) should be fully explored. As far as possible, time permitting, the various market segments should be tested by direct mail and the nonproductive lists dropped, thus ensuring maximum mileage for the society's promotional dollar.

• Promotional material should be mailed repeatedly to the productive lists of potential subscribers. A list that generates 3% response from a first mailing this month will generate another 3% next month, for the same product. A good list should be mailed until the return ceases to be cost-effective, discontinued for six months or so, and then reactivated. In summary, direct mail can be used as an effective market research tool, at the same time as it sells subscriptions, sight unseen, to your new journal.

OTHER ELEMENTS IN THE MARKETING MIX

Space Advertising

Space advertising (running ads in journals in related fields) is a useful adjunct to direct mail. It accomplishes somewhat different results, and generally its results are more difficult to measure than those from direct mail. However, a well-designed, professionally written advertisement will gain the attention of people (legion in the professions) who never read direct mail. In professional fields, space ads also tend to lend credibility to a new journal. Finally, space advertising used in conjunction with other promotional media helps boost product awareness.

Measuring the results of space advertising is tough: even running a coupon at the foot of the ad does not guarantee a traceable response, since many scientists are understandably unwilling to cut bits out of their professional publications. Some journals, moreover, will not accept coupon ads, so it is a good idea to check such restrictions *before* the ad is made up.

Finally, although the cost per thousand for paid space advertising is much lower than for direct mail, the response rate is much lower too, in most cases. As a rule of thumb, not more than 10% of the total marketing budget should be allotted to paid space advertising.

Display at Exhibits

Displaying either the new or the established journal at exhibits held in conjunction with professional meetings is an excellent adjunct to direct mail and space advertising. Often journals are known by their physical characteristics; product recognition is extremely important as a journal vies for its share of attention in a world crowded with competitors. The kind of exposure a journal can get at a meeting is unmatched: the hands-on approach is a proven circulation builder.

Of course there are drawbacks, particularly the uncontrolled nature of the exposure: who stops by your booth and picks up the journal is entirely fortuitous. The other major drawback is cost. These days, exhibit space seldom costs less than $1000 for a major convention display. Add to that the cost of sending personnel to run the booth, the cost of the booth or display itself, and the overhead, and the actual cost of this kind of first-rate exposure is very high.

The middle ground—exhibiting only at conventions where your society already has a booth, or where you can exchange booth space with a sister society, or where you can participate in a cooperative (multipublisher) display of some sort—promises high-quality exposure for your journal at a more affordable price.

RENEWAL STRATEGIES

"Once you've got'em, never let'em go" should be the slogan of all journal publishers. The natural attrition rate of 5–10% in nonrenewals to scientific journals is the result of people retiring, dying, or changing professions. In institutional circulation, nonrenewals are almost always the result of budget cuts. The continued promotion of the established journal is aimed at counterbalancing the attrition factor and at adding new subscriptions on top of the annual turnaround. But the core of any journal operation is the renewing subscriber, and it is essential to maximize the effectiveness of the renewal effort.

Those who subscribe to nonprofessional journals like *Time* are aware of the immense effort the publisher makes to retain our subscription business. Renewal notices are accompanied by letters that, in sequence, cajole, bribe, intimidate, plead. If you do not respond after seven to nine renewal attempts, your subscription expires. But, a month or so later, you begin to receive new mailings, soliciting your subscription as a *new* subscriber. In other words, you are on their list!

Normally, in scientific publishing, two to four renewal notices are adequate to reach the 85–95% renewal (commercial publishers, in consumer markets such as *Time*, experience much lower renewal rates of 60–75%). Nevertheless, an explanatory ("sales") letter sent with the renewal bill is helpful, particularly as first notices go out some six months before the expiration date. An explanation why the bill is sent so early may increase the percentage of subscribers renewing from the first notice and reduce the costs of subsequent renewal efforts. Also, a "Bill me" option on the early renewal notices will help in getting a commitment to renew from the subscriber, even though payment may not be received for a few more months, and formal invoices will be needed. Finally, do not overlook expired subscriptions. Every effort should be made to get those who were once faithful to return to the flock. Maintain a list of expires, and mail promotional material to the former subscribers as a matter of course every few months.

COST-EFFECTIVE PROMOTIONAL TECHNIQUES

In conclusion, a checklist is presented of ways to make the most of each promotional dollar.

• Maintain in-house lists of buyers of related products and services and of expired subscriptions.

• Set up list exchange agreements with other societies in related disciplines.

- Use promotional brochures as stuffers with office correspondence, related mailings, and mailings the sustaining members may be glad to have your society participate in.
- Check into all of the free catalog and directory listings to which you are entitled as a society or association publisher.
- Maximize the journal's exposure at meetings of your own society; send non-member registrants special information about the journal.
- Check into the society's nonprofit status. Bulk rate postage at the time this chapter was prepared was 5.9¢ per piece for nonprofit mail (501–C3), 10.9¢ per piece for other 3rd class mail.
- If going to the expense of printing a brochure, make it as all-purpose as possible. Often, however, a simple sales letter will be more effective than a costly brochure.
- When contemplating direct mail promotion, always plan *every* detail of your mailing in advance, and call in, at the outset, the experts who can save you money: writers, graphic artists, printers, mail list brokers, mailing houses.
- Test large unknown lists.
- Set up mechanisms for recording the response to direct mail.
- If something works, STICK WITH IT!

Subject Index